Ryan and Jeffrey are two guys who love baseball, but together they give us a book that is bigger than the game. Ryan courageously tells us what it feels like to have it all – looks, money, a dream job – and still feel lost. In his despair, though, he finds out what is important. This is a heartfelt book that will challenge you to think a bit about what happiness really means.

– Joe Posnanski

Sports Illustrated

Ryan has always been one of my favorite people in baseball, and now I admire him even more for his bravery in sharing his problem with depression so publicly, and for his willingness to help others. This is a great story about a remarkable guy.

– Jim Souhan

Minneapolis Star Tribune

When Ryan told me, on the air, about driving home from Royals games with tears pouring down his cheeks as he tried to call his mother, I was struck by his honesty and wished I could have done something to help. He has fought a courageous battle with depression and kept his soul intact. Now, maybe his words can help others who are feeling isolated or alone.

– Rory Markas

Los Angeles Angels radio and television broadcaster

The Shame of Me

One Man's Journey to Depression and Back

By Ryan Lefebvre with Jeffrey Flanagan

Foreword by Mike Sweeney

www.ascendbooks.com

10 9 8 7 6 5 4 3 2 1

Printed in the United States of America

ISBN-13: 978-0-9841130-2-6

ISBN-10: 0-9841130-2-9

Library of Congress Cataloging-in-Publications Data
Available Upon Request

Editor: Lee Stuart

Design: The Covington Group

www.ascendbooks.com

DEDICATIONS

For Mom. After surviving a bloody war with depression herself, she returned to the battlefield to rescue me. This story would have a different ending without her.

– Ryan Lefebvre

I'd like to thank Ryan for having the courage to tell his story and enough faith in my judgment to allow me to steer this story toward its final form. It was a pleasure to help.

– Jeffrey Flanagan

FOREWORD

In September of 1995, I got the opportunity to live out my childhood dreams when I was called up to the big leagues. This life-changing invitation to play baseball in "The Show" was given to me by the Kansas City Royals, the team that drafted me as a 17-year-old catcher from Southern California. Playing in the Major Leagues was everything I ever dreamed it would be, and then some! I was no longer making $850 per month, taking 13-hour bus rides and eating peanut butter and jelly sandwiches served with wooden tongue depressors on Wonder Bread. I was now sharing a locker room with guys whose baseball cards and posters adorned my bedroom walls as a boy. I was living the dream of every American boy who laced up a pair of cleats in a Little League game or played catch with his Dad. And life was good. No, it was great!

In the same year of 1995, there was a young man who was living out his childhood dreams in Minneapolis, Minnesota. As the son of Major League manager Jim Lefebvre, young Ryan aspired to some day play in the "bigs" like his Daddy. As a collegiate ballplayer, Ryan starred for the University of Minnesota Golden Gophers where he was a three-time, all-Big Ten Conference centerfielder and was named league MVP in 1993. After college, Ryan played professionally in the Cleveland Indians organization as a centerfielder but soon he realized the quickest road to the big leagues was not with a bat and ball but with a microphone and a smile. Ryan received his chance to live out that big-league dream when he was given the role of television broadcaster for the Minnesota Twins. Ryan quickly established himself as one of the most respected and knowledgeable broadcasters in the game. He was living the dream of every communications major in the world. And life for him was good. No, it was great!

In the fall of 1995, two men were living out their respective dreams. Both were well on their way to stardom, but there was one problem: Neither had a map or a compass for their journey and both had a long way to go before they reached their destination. Both were on different roads leading to the same place. In a way, they were two runaway trains destined to collide – only the collision would not lead to destruction but to direction. And it would be good. No, it would be great!

The spring training of 1999 is one I will remember for the rest of my life. While I was in Baseball City, Florida, the spring training home of the Royals, my heart exploded when I was introduced to our new radio broadcaster. I remember meeting Ryan Lefebvre like it was yesterday because it was rare to have "The Radio Guy" as a young, handsome, ex-ballplayer who liked to skateboard, lift weights and go to Mass in his spare time. What I remember most about that day was looking into Ryan's eyes and being taken back as I recalled the Proverb, "The eyes are the windows to the soul." I saw such life, excitement and beauty in those eyes but I also saw so much pain. What I didn't know that day was that I would see a transformation take place in those eyes and in the life of my new friend over the next 10 years. The transformation you will read about in this book is amazing.

Over the past 10 years, Ryan and I have experienced some incredible highs and lows that made our friendship more of a brotherhood. Many people over the years have asked me, "Who are your closest friends on the team?" Some would chuckle when I'd mention the name Ryan Lefebvre in the middle of Joe Randa, Jermaine Dye, Jeremy Affeldt and Brent Mayne. Today, I'm so proud to call Ryan Lefebvre my friend and my brother. As you get to know the life of this modern-day saint, I pray God will give you an accurate portrait of this man's heart through the pages that make up this book.

Most people who read a book and then watch the

movie about that book will often rave that the book was much better. I'm sure if someone were to one day make a movie of the book you are holding in your hands, you'd probably say the same.

Me, well I'm the lucky one: I've read this amazing book and seen firsthand the journey of a courageous man that a movie cannot capture. As you embark on this emotional journey of pain and redemption with Ryan, may you be filled with the joy and pride that this man's life and heart have brought to me.

– **Mike Sweeney**

Proverbs 18:24 *"A man of many companions may come to ruin, but there is a friend who sticks closer than a brother."*

TABLE OF CONTENTS

The Darkness

I am alone, trembling on the floor in my closet. It is dark. There is no sound. I picture the cars driving away. They are leaving…that image. I begin to sob, breaking the silence. They are leaving. I am alone.

I don't know what happened. How did I get to this point?

I stare straight ahead, straight at the darkness. Minutes pass by, maybe hours. I don't know. I don't remember. There is no reason to get up, no reason to leave the closet. I am empty.

Something is dying inside of me.

I sit crouched against the wall, my hands on my shins. I rock forward, my forehead taps against my knees. I am so alone. So damn alone.

Where is my Mom? I want my Mom.

I've been here before, felt this way before. Alone. Abandoned. Why did they leave? Why do I ache like this? Tears drip down my cheeks. I feel the tears hit my legs. It is all I feel.

What's going to happen to me?

The tears finally stop. They always do. Then the next stage begins. Pain gives way to fear. I am scared, really scared. I am losing it. I know that.

Is anybody going to find me?

I am staying right here, in this closet. I am not moving. I don't want to move. I don't want any lights turned on. I don't want the sunlight. I will stay here, in the darkness. It is safe in the dark.

Is anyone coming for me?

Pain and fear take their turns with me. They fight for control of me. I have lost. I know that. This is bad, really bad.

Make this stop.

My heart starts to beat faster. I know I am in trouble. I can't make this stop, not anymore. Not this time. All I can think about is Mom. Oh, God, I'm in trouble.

Where is she? Why isn't she here?

My Mom is 800 miles away. It is August 7, 2005. I am 34 years old and I don't know if I want to live anymore.

Emptiness

To most people, I'm sure I didn't fit the profile of a person who would suffer from anxiety and depression. On the surface, my life probably seemed pretty blessed. I was 34 years old, not bad looking, owned a wonderful house on a lake, had great friends, and worked a dream job to most sports fans – television and radio announcer for a Major League Baseball team, the Kansas City Royals. It was more than a decent life, right? But none of that seemed to matter to me, and it certainly didn't matter to my disorder.

I realize now that I had been battling depression my whole life. Thoughts of ending it all were nothing new to me. I'm really not sure why I never acted upon those thoughts. What stopped me? Was I too afraid? I know there were times I was low enough to do it. But something always seemed to pull me back. But on the night of August 7, 2005, I was close. I mean really close.

On that night, I sat alone in my house, feeling completely separated from the world. I will always remember the overpowering feeling from that night, through all my sobs, of how much I simply wanted my Mom. Here I was, a 34-year-old man in his 11th season broadcasting Major League Baseball, crying out for his Mom. How did it come to this?

I knew something was terribly wrong with me. I had experienced the grip of sadness before, but nothing as overwhelming as the one from that night. I knew that night I wasn't going to crawl away. I had no idea I was capable of breaking down so completely.

The trigger for my breakdown was perhaps the most innocent-appearing event one could imagine. August 7 started out with a day game against the Oakland A's. Afterward, my boss, David Witty, and his family joined me and a girlfriend on the lake. We couldn't have asked for a better day for playing on the lake. It was a typical hot, sunny, August day in Kansas City. What better time for some swimming, water-skiing, and tubing? But an afternoon of watching a very happy Witty family enjoy time together on the lake threw me into a strange darkness. Their happiness actually made me feel uncomfortable. It was a glaring reminder of how far I was from that same joy and contentment. I knew I was light years away from that peace. True, I was smiling on the outside that afternoon. But I could sense the darkness brewing inside.

Later in the evening, I stood in the driveway as the Witty family drove off. And then, I stood in the driveway again, as my girlfriend drove away. The pain started to grow as I walked back toward the front door. As the taillights faded away at the end of my street, I turned to enter my empty house. Within seconds it seemed, I felt frighteningly alone. My home suddenly felt like an empty department store. And I felt like a young child trying to find my Mom as the lights went out one at a time. I got scared. And like the child in the empty department store, I needed to find a place where I could just curl up and cry. That's when I headed to my closet.

In my life, the lights had been going off one by one

for years. On August 7, 2005, at about 10 o'clock, the power went out altogether.

Morning After

I finally fell asleep that night, at least for a few hours. I probably can credit the most intense round of crying of my life for allowing me to get any sleep at all. As you may know, there are certain physiological benefits to crying. First, you release a lot of built-up emotion, which makes you feel better. Second, the act of crying – and especially the intense crying I experienced that night – physically wears you out. In a sense, crying calms you down, acting like a natural sedative. I was more calm. But I was still broken into many pieces.

I didn't know it at the time but I was suffering from depression. I had been for years. This early in the process, however, I was only bewildered by this unprecedented emotional pain. This pain woke me up again about 5 AM. Waking up around this time was somewhat of a common occurrence for me during this period of my life. It's one of the few advantages of depression: you no longer need an alarm clock. I knew what time it would be before I even rolled over to look at the clock. Sure enough, it was always 5 AM.

What was different this time, though, was waking up

to some searing mental anguish. I used to wake up to some general sadness and normally, shortly after waking, I would always be reminded of whatever it was on my mind that had triggered the depression. Sleep had always been just a temporary chalkboard eraser for me. Feelings of melancholy would fill the day and a few hours of sleep would erase everything, at least momentarily. Not this time. This time, I felt hollow and frightened and broken the moment I awoke, even before rolling over to look at the clock. I knew this was a horrible indication that I was in deep psychological trouble. The agony of the night before slept right beside me the whole night. It was awake before I was, waiting to greet me.

I tried to go back to sleep and perhaps did so for a few minutes. It's hard to remember. The real alarm clock, not the one in my head, went off at 7 AM. This is also the alarm clock for my two dogs. They know the music means it's time for a walk and some breakfast. On this morning, though, I was in no mood or condition to go for our regular morning walk. I let them out to the backyard briefly, fed them, and then went back to bed. That was about all I could muster that morning.

Amazingly, despite all the tears from the night before, my body still managed to produce more tears that morning. I'm not sure why, but that amazed me.

I remember thinking that I must have an enormous teardrop tank capacity. The sobbing returned just as intensely as it had been the night before.

I kept thinking to myself: How did I get to this point? What in the world was wrong with me? Why did I feel this way? I know this sounds shallow but at that very moment I did a quick inventory of all the materialistic things I had acquired by age 34, things most men probably only dream of having. I had a great job, a four-bedroom house on a lake, two expensive cars in the garage, and a boat and a jet-ski down at my dock. I made a nice income that allowed me to do most everything I wanted in life. I was dating a former beauty queen. When I was younger, this was the life I had dreamed of. And yet, here I was, completely miserable. I had worked hard and I had achieved and I had accumulated and yet, I had nothing. I was a mess.

I had put myself on this path, that much I knew. When I was 23, I decided I wanted to become the youngest announcer in Major League Baseball. That was the goal. I was determined. And that achievement came quickly, the very next year (1995), when I hooked on with the Minnesota Twins. The next mission was obtaining a substantial income level. I achieved that in 1998 (27 years old) when I took a job with the Kansas City Royals.

Rather quickly, my materialistic needs started to get filled. I bought my first luxury car in 1999. Then at the age of 29, I bought a house on Lake Winnebago, Missouri, several miles southeast of metropolitan Kansas City. I was certain this was part of the road to happiness. I had arrived. Now it was time for the rest of the world to take notice, I figured. Sure, I also assumed that happiness would include finding the right woman to love. But with all that I had become and all that I had achieved, maybe I just figured she would find me. I guess you might say I had some entitlement issues.

Something else I remembered thinking on the morning after August 7 was just how much my life had changed in a relatively short time. I used to love the idea of playing on the lake during the day, then announcing baseball games at night. I fished with a neighbor on off-days. I played golf on the team's road trips. I took acting lessons in the fall and winter. I wrote short stories and screenplays. I took painting lessons and enjoyed spending hours in my art room, just spilling some creativity onto the canvas. I was learning to play the piano. I had some CDs to teach myself Spanish. I played ice hockey once a week. I hung out regularly with my Kansas City friends and had visitors from college staying at the lake for weekends of fun. I was a man of balance, or so I thought.

I could make people laugh. What the hell happened to me?

I suddenly realized I hadn't fished or painted in two years. No more acting classes or ice hockey games in the off-season. I hadn't written a story or a screenplay in two years. I hadn't touched the piano. I had forgotten all of the Spanish I had learned. I hardly ever saw my friends. I played golf maybe twice a year. It was clear to me that I'd lost that person I had aspired to be. Or maybe that wasn't really me, either. Anyway, somewhere along the line, I transformed into something else. Depression had taken control of my life and stripped me of everything I enjoyed doing. (Actually, as I learned later, depression had always been there, just waiting in the wings.)

Regarding the morning after, on August 8, I did catch one break. The Royals had an off-day that day. At least I wouldn't have to face anybody at the stadium. I did, however, have to host my annual charity event, Gloves for Kids. Several Royals players were gracious enough to spend a couple of hours signing autographs at a local sporting goods store to raise money for underprivileged youth baseball programs in Kansas City. It is a program and an event I am very proud of. But I wanted nothing to do with Gloves for Kids on August 8, 2005. I was terrified. What if I had a breakdown at the store in front of everyone? I didn't want to be exposed. I knew it was possible. I had to do something to prevent that from happening.

The first step back

The one thing I knew I needed to do on August 8 was call my Mom. I didn't know where else to turn. And I knew she might have an idea of what I should do. I tried my best, through yet even more tears, to explain what I was going through. She tried her best to find out just what was wrong with me. Naturally, I couldn't give her any logical answers. Having suffered through clinical depression herself, however, she could sense my symptoms. She knew that this wasn't just a momentary bit of sadness that most people endure in the normal course of a life. She recognized almost immediately this was different. She recognized that I was in serious trouble.

She insisted that I talk to a professional immediately...as in that day! I can't remember all the details of that conversation but I do recall my Mom being very assertive about my seeking immediate professional help. She said I needed to call anyone I could think of who might recommend a psychologist or psychiatrist. She told me to start dialing the second we hung up and then to call her back in 10 minutes. She was adamant that I come up with a plan, a rescue plan so to speak.

Doing as I was told, I dialed the phone. I called my neighbor and friend, Julee. She is married to an orthopedic surgeon. I thought perhaps her husband might know someone I could talk to. I tried to explain to Julee what was going on but I had some difficulty because I wasn't exactly sure myself. I just remember her saying, "My gosh, you sound terrible." I'm sure I wasn't making much sense so I politely ended the conversation and said I'd call her back. As soon as I hung up the phone with Julee, I called my chiropractor, Emily Long. I told her I was having an extremely tough day and needed to talk to a professional. It's not easy to explain to people that you feel like you're cracking up. I imagined the conversation: "Hey, this is Ryan. How are you? The kids? Great. Hey, I was just wondering, since I'm about to go insane and all, do you happen to know any head doctor I could chat with? Oh, you do? Fabulous! Thanks, so much. Let's do lunch sometime."

I guess my voice sounded frantic enough that even without going into too many details, Emily immediately sensed my dire situation and suggested a therapist who had helped her family through a tragedy. Emily and her husband are wonderful people and I had no doubt she was recommending someone who could help me. I called the pager number and left a message for a Dale

Williamson who announced she was a "licensed professional counselor and registered play therapist." Hmm. A "play therapist?" At this point I was willing to talk to a licensed or registered anybody. I can't remember what I said but apparently my words made a strong impression because my call was returned in a matter of minutes and Dale agreed to meet me that afternoon.

I called my Mom and then Julee to tell them the news and spent the next several hours in bed ignoring the telephone and the rest of the world.

When the time came for me to get dressed and go to my therapy, I spent some time standing in my living room looking out at the lake. August 8 was another beautiful day in Kansas City, and the lake was busy with adults and kids enjoying the weather and the water. I felt somewhat relieved just looking at the scene. I guess, at least for a moment, I was reminded of why I wanted to live there in the first place. I thought about all of the good times I'd had on the lake with friends. This gave me a very small sense of peace and hope.

My Mom

I hope I never have to single-handedly raise a child, as my Mom had to. Yet, despite the obstacles of doing so, she raised me to be a man of integrity. Lying wasn't an option, responsibility was demanded, and affection was abundant. We traveled the world together, she attended most of my athletic events, taught me how to sell Christmas cards during a school fundraiser (changing my approach based on who I was selling to), made sure I spoke proper English, and tried to get me to become an avid reader. For several years after her separation from my Dad, it was just the two of us.

Mom was a college-graduated, world-traveled, multi-lingual former model. That's what people saw on

> Mom was a college-graduated, world-traveled, multi-lingual former model. That's what people saw on the outside. On the inside, at this point in her life, she was a betrayed, divorced, single mother in her early 30s who was trying to figure out what she was going to do with the rest of her existence.

the outside. On the inside, at this point in her life, she was a betrayed, divorced, single mother in her early 30s who was trying to figure out what she was going to do with the rest of her existence. This was not the life she had in mind.

This was the 1970s, the "me" era, and this was southern California (the birthplace of "all about me"). People partied and my Mom was no exception, and in her mind, she had her reasons.

I was too young to know exactly what was going on during my Mom's parties. But I knew whatever was happening, it probably wasn't good. People showed up because my Mom was beautiful, smart, and cool. She was the star of the group, at least that was the appearance on the outside.

It usually began with my Mom having a couple of friends over for a bottle of wine. I'd head off to bed and I always remember asking my Mom when she was going to bed. She would tell me that she was going to stay up just a little bit longer but that she wouldn't be up too late. I would ask her to promise me that she would be going to bed soon because I could sense a party in the works. I didn't understand what alcohol was and why it was being used by my Mom and her friends, but I knew that after several hours they changed in physical appearance. I didn't know what intoxicated meant, but I knew what it looked like. I knew these parties weren't good for her and I just wanted her to go to sleep. I guess I was trying to protect her, in some way.

Quite often, I'd be asleep for a few hours and then I would awaken to the sound of loud music and equally loud conversation. I knew this meant it was going to be a long night. There were a few rare occasions when I couldn't sleep through the noise and gathered up enough courage to walk out of my room, in my pajamas, and stand in front of the party in protest. I wouldn't have to say a word. My mere presence seemed powerful, as a bunch of intoxicated adults realized their noise had stirred a cute little boy out of bed. Perhaps I represented reality to them. I was the ultimate buzz-kill. Instant sobriety. I knew I never needed to say a single word. I just needed to show up. Perhaps some of the people there had a kid just like me at home. I was the sobering effect, providing instant guilt. I didn't pull my protests often at first, but when I did, three things would normally follow after I appeared: First, it would get deathly quiet. Second, my Mom would jump off the couch and run up to me to make sure I was all right. I would explain that I couldn't sleep through the noise and she would take me back to my room, tuck me into bed and promise that she would do something about the noise. Again, I would ask her to promise that she would be going to bed soon. One time, some guy I never saw before (or after) yelled out, "Hey, man, who's the kid?" My Mom quickly snapped, "He's my son, asshole." And third, the party began to break up.

I never was physically threatened during any of these parties. That much I want to make clear. I feared more for my mother. I guess I figured that if she wasn't safe, then I wasn't safe, either. As I look back, I understand that the parties left some emotional wounds. Without realizing it at the time, I felt my Mom was choosing her friends, the loud music and conversation, and "that feeling" over me. Perhaps this is where I began to feel detached. I may have misinterpreted it as being abandoned. Anyway, because of that, I grew up despising alcohol. As I got older, I began to spend weekends with my fraternal grandparents. My grandfather was a binge alcoholic and I was witness to some all-nighters that kept everyone on pins and needles. I felt uncomfortable when my Dad had "a beer" with some pals. Even to this day, an innocent mention of opening a bottle of wine causes me to imagine something much worse.

Long before I was ever introduced to the concept of self-medication, I knew my Mom was hosting these parties for all the wrong reasons. And she had some reasons.

As a young woman, she left Wisconsin because she loved to travel and had many places she wanted to see. She became a flight attendant and lived in New York City and Chicago. It was during that time that she caught the attention of an attractive and famous Major League baseball player – my father, Jim Lefebvre. She married him and moved to his hometown of Los Angeles. They were the toast of the town. She traveled to all of the big cities with her husband. She spent her days shopping with other players' wives, then watched the games at night in what is known in big-league circles as the "trophy section" of the ballparks. That's the area, usually right behind the dugouts, where the players store their "trophy" wives or girlfriends. Newspaper photographers loved her, and her picture often seemed to show up in the sports pages. A few years after she married, she became a mother and was able to take this perceived charmed life to another level. Photographers

My Mom was an incredible source of strength for me throughout my ordeal.

Photo courtesy of Ryan Lefebvre

now were capturing a happy family, not just a happy couple. This was her destiny, she figured.

Then, one day, it was all gone. The only thing about her in the newspaper was a short item about her divorce. She was just another pretty face in a big city filled with pretty faces. And she was saddled with the stigma of Single Mom. For her, there was a mountain of hurt. And there was a child to raise. This wasn't the life she signed up for but she accepted the responsibility.

As I look back on those years now, I realize that Mom worked very hard to support both of us. At times I attended private schools that required expensive tuition. Because of her hard work and success, she was offered career advances and new opportunities in other cities.

Years later I would learn that she didn't accept any of those positions because she didn't want to remove me from my grandparents and my Dad. So she chose me over her career. We enjoyed many adventures together and there were many precious mother-son moments. But there was something about those parties that first opened up a wound. It would take many years for me to even realize there was a wound. That had to happen before any healing started.

Dale

I arrived at Dale's office at 4 PM. She introduced herself and closed the door behind us. She was a middle-aged, short lady with a trendy, blond hairstyle. She was dressed very casually and had a very confident manner about her. It wasn't arrogance. It was actually very comforting. It made me feel like I was with someone who knew what she was doing.

Actually, it wasn't even Dale's office. She rented an office from someone, so all of the pictures on the desk and walls were of someone else's family. I did have some prior experience with psychologists on a very limited basis. It wasn't quite like the movies, but the offices I had been to had couches and big, comfortable chairs. Not this office. This was more like a principal's office. I had several experiences in places like that.

She explained that she worked for the local school district as a counselor but used this place for her private practice. She pulled up a chair for me facing the desk. I sat down. She sat behind the desk facing me, pulled out a box of Kleenex, placed it in front of me and said rather businesslike, "So, tell me what's going on."

After grabbing about 17 sheets of Kleenex and burying my face for about three minutes I finally declared, "I don't know." Here's where the professional separates herself from the supportive friend. Without hesitation Dale responded, "Then why are you crying?" It seemed like an elementary response but the tone of her voice suggested to me that she was really saying: I'm a professional. You are a mess. So let's try again. What's going on?

She wasn't being insensitive, she was trying to help me and unless I gave her some information, we'd be wasting each other's time.

I began by telling her that I felt lost. I had spent most of the day realizing that I no longer had any balance in my life. I had become an extremely reclusive and lonely person, and I did it to myself. I was spiraling down from a life of fullness to one of emptiness. In the eyes of most everyone else, I was a young man with so much going for him. Finding a willing female to settle down and start a family should be easy. Yet I had become Royals broadcaster Ryan Lefebvre and that was it. I had no other identity. I had no other outlets. Nothing seemed interesting anymore. I told her how watching the Witty family hit me like a dagger to the heart. I had accomplished most everything I thought would make me happy. A wife and family were next on the list, and I realized how far away I was from that. I didn't know what I wanted. I had lost myself.

I had become Royals broadcaster Ryan Lefebvre and that was it. I had no other identity.

Dale was confident that this had very little to do with finding a wife and starting a family. She said the emotions I was experiencing were disproportionate to the event that triggered the emotions. There was a much deeper issue.

She asked me to list all of the thoughts bouncing around my head that made me feel as though I was empty and without purpose. I told her, "I'm all alone. I feel like I've accomplished nothing. I've become nothing. Nobody is going to want to be with me. Who wants to be with a nothing? I'm lost and I don't know where to go."

With each of my statements, Dale would look me directly in the eyes and ask, "Ryan, is that true?"

When I took the time to think about what I was saying, I realized how ridiculous I sounded. After sheepishly realizing my statements were based mostly on emotion, Dale jumped back in, "Ryan, those are lies. I know you are feeling really terrible right now, but let's begin with separating the facts from the lies."

By doing so she gracefully intertwined her secular education and our shared Christian faith, reinstating my beliefs about the truth of my current situation and the truth about whether I was really alone, now or before.

This was a good start.

Dale didn't disagree with my assessment of losing balance in my life but she wanted to know why I chose to narrow my focus the way I had. Why had I suddenly put all of my eggs in the wife-and-family basket?

"Ryan, are you afraid of being alone?" Dale asked very matter-of-factly. "Do you feel abandoned?"

Her questions cut right through me. I knew this wasn't the time to play tough and act as though I was too old to feel this way. This hurt was too much to ignore. I was also too weak to lie. But I didn't say anything. My head fell again into my hands as I came face to face with my demons.

My therapy was underway.

A Major League Dad

It wasn't until much later in life that I realized the effect on me of never seeing my Mom and Dad love each other. I was 18 months old when they separated for the first time and they were officially divorced by the time I was 5. When I would compare war stories with other kids about our parents' divorces, the conventional wisdom was that I was spared most of the pain because I was too young to understand. They'd say: "At least you didn't have to live through the arguments and the crying, and having to ask why Daddy doesn't live with us anymore." To this day, I still believe some of this to be true. However, as it was explained to me in later years through therapy, it is likely there was a level of damage done regardless. The lack of any love and respect displayed by my parents toward each other could have contributed to my own sense of emptiness and fears of abandonment. It's not like children immediately notice anything wrong with their parents' behavior toward each other (unless there's obvious physical or verbal abuse) because, for children, there's very little to compare that behavior to. But when I became old enough to really take notice of my parents' behavior, I realized I never once heard them compliment each other. Not once. I never saw them smile at each other genuinely, let alone hug and kiss. When my great-grandmother, Louisa Girard, died when I was a freshman in high school, my Dad comforted my Mom as she wept by the casket. That image still sticks with me. That was the first time – the only time – I saw any type of affection between the two people who brought me into this world. That moment of affection was short-lived.

I do know that some of my fondest childhood memories involve my Dad. He wasn't so much a true or traditional father as he was a buddy. A baseball buddy. A sports buddy.

I was aware that my mom and step-father loathed him, perhaps because of his lack of skills at parenting, or his lack of interest in it.

I guess his shortcomings didn't matter to me at the time. I would spend weekends, holidays, and parts of summers with my Dad as I was growing up. In the late 1970s, he lived near us in southern California and I would visit him on the weekends during the baseball off-season. This was during the football season and we would spend our afternoons watching games on television and throwing the football during halftime. There was a deli down the street from his apartment in Marina del Rey and we would routinely order submarine sandwiches and Aspen soda. As we watched the games and ate, Dad would spontaneously call out quarterback signals, "Ready...blue 92...blue 92...hutt, hutt, hutt." This meant that I would jump off the couch and run an impromptu pass pattern through his apartment and he would throw me the Nerf football just far enough so I had to make a leaping or diving catch. If I made the catch, there would be an end zone celebration. If I didn't make the catch, Dad would break out in mock rage, "How did you drop that ball? You've got to be kidding me! We lost the game!" I would respond with mock anguish. It was great fun. And it was just the two of us.

We never once went fishing or camping. We never discussed feelings about girls or life or anything like that. That wasn't his strength. His specialty was baseball and sports, so that's how we bonded. His way of telling me he loved me was having me at the ballpark, which is where I spent the better part of my summers as an adolescent. My first real "road trip" to visit him was in 1978 when he managed a minor league team in the Los Angeles Dodgers organization located in Lethbridge, Alberta. I was 7 years old that summer and it was my first stab at being a bat boy. Two things stand out about my first evening in Lethbridge. First of all, my Dad was ejected from the game after a heated discussion with the home plate umpire. I was not more than 20 feet away and got to hear what was actually said during one of these manager/umpire screaming matches I'd seen so often on television. It was an education for a 7-year-old. It definitely strengthened my vocabulary, and taught me the economy of language, such as condensing god-damn-son-of-a-bitch-shit-for-brains into one word with a minimum of syllables. Even though it was summer and school was out, that was one of the best vocabulary lessons I ever received.

Secondly, going to games and watching them on television whetted my appetite to be a bat boy. I thought it was so cool to watch kids run out to home plate to collect bats or replenish the home plate umpire's baseball stash. The coolest, in my mind, was running along the screen behind home plate to retrieve a foul ball. So in Lethbridge, I couldn't wait for my first opportunity. As I was processing some of the words that my Dad hurled at the umpire before his early trip to the showers, I saw a ball roll to the screen. This was my chance. I bolted up from my small wooden stool and raced to the ball. I must have been pretty quick because I got there right before the catcher did. Apparently it wasn't a foul ball; it was a wild pitch and I officially interfered with a live ball. Luckily, the catcher was on my Dad's team so he wasn't about to say anything inappropriate to the manager's kid, especially the currently enraged manager's kid. That same catcher, Dann Bilardello, eventually made it to the big leagues. He also took me to the movie Grease during that summer of 1978.

I made my Major League debut as a bat boy in 1980, my Dad's first year with the San Francisco Giants as their batting coach. It was June 27, 1980, at Candlestick Park in San Francisco. It was less than a year after my

Dad's infamous incident when he punched Dodgers' manager Tommy Lasorda in the nose during an argument away from the ballpark. Not long after that, my Dad left the Dodgers and accepted the batting-coach job with the rival Giants. The switch in organizations for my Dad actually had a profound effect on me, too. You have to understand that I was a born-and-raised Dodgers fan. I was now nine years old and dealing with my first major dilemma: Which team held my loyalties? On the night when I made my major-league debut as a bat boy, the Dodgers were in town, which meant I was meeting new players with the Giants while getting reacquainted with the Dodgers' players. I was wearing my brand new Giants uniform, but my favorite team was still my hometown Dodgers. What was a 9-year-old to do?

Back in those days, both teams and both cities braced themselves for a Giants/Dodgers series, especially in San Francisco. There were fights in the stands, fights on the field, fans running onto the field, fans setting uniforms ablaze, full beer cups launched onto players' heads, you name it. The fans hated each other and the players hated each other. I had never seen anything like it before in my life. It was absolute chaos. But to a 9-year-old debuting as a bat boy, it was pure excitement. And without my Dad, I never would have experienced that excitement. That's the night I officially shifted my allegiance from the Dodgers to the Giants. That's also the night I learned that your loyalties lie with the uniform you're wearing at the time. I guess that's true in life, too. When I was with my Dad, my loyalties were with him.

I spent the next 12 summers visiting my Dad wherever his career took him. He went from Giants batting coach to Giants minor league manager to Oakland A's third base coach to Seattle Mariners manager to Chicago Cubs manager. I continued my bat-boy career and got to experience baseball in many large cities and many small towns. I hung out around the clubhouse, shagged fly balls during batting practice, played cards with the players on the team plane, and spent time with my Dad. He would have his routine at the ballpark and I would have mine. Afterward, we would drive home and talk about the game. Sometimes we would go to the ballpark early the following day and he would throw me batting practice on the field. It was a wonderful journey. I bashed forearms with Mark McGwire and Jose Canseco. I took batting practice at Wrigley Field, Fenway Park, and Tiger Stadium. I was interviewed on national television by Harry Caray. This was big, big stuff for a kid. I had some amazing and wonderful experiences, thanks to my Dad. But he and I never had a traditional father-son relationship.

Up until the age of 18 or so, I thought being Jim

Lefebvre's son was fine. I knew it wasn't great but I didn't complain any more than other boys did about their fathers who were in the Major Leagues. He'd forget birthdays from time to time and he wasn't all that great at fulfilling promises. But I accepted him the way he was. My Dad married my step-mother, Ruth, in 1982. I was 11. They began having children in 1984. From their marriage, I have two half-sisters and one half-brother. Later on, I was encouraged by my Dad to sleep at the stadium in the locker room when I visited him during the summer. He would tell me that "it would just be easier that way." As the years went on, I knew I was being pushed away from his "real" family. But I decided to cope with it the best way I knew how: Have some fun. So, I would stay up all night in the locker rooms playing baseball games, chewing tobacco, and yes, even drinking beer. I was making the best of the situation, or so I thought. I felt I was becoming a lower priority in my Dad's world. I began to see how other kids spent more quality time with their fathers. I still enjoyed hanging out at the ballpark with my Dad but we no longer had the bonding time after the games. I spent less and less time with him each year. Summer at the ballpark became much more of a personal party time than spending time with my Dad.

Did I blame my Dad for that? I did for a long time. There were several years when we hardly spoke and I blamed him for most anything that was lacking in my life. He wasn't around and that was on him. If he wanted to spend all of his time with his new family and cast me aside, I reasoned, that was fine. I could make it without him. That attitude only went so far.

One day, I discovered that forgiveness was a better solution than lifelong resentment. As I hoped people could forgive me for my shortcomings, I understood I must do the same for others, especially my parents. I began to understand that the only connection he had with my alcoholic grandfather was sports. There was no example for him to follow, so he turned to sports as a means of experiencing joy and avoiding pain. When my parents first separated in 1972, my Dad's Major League career was coming to an end.

He played just 70 games for the Los Angeles Dodgers that season and struggled to maintain a .200 batting average. Yet he was only 30 years old and not ready to give up on the only thing he wanted to do, the only thing he knew how to do. Already dealing with a crumbling marriage and now a crumbling career, he signed on with the Japanese Lotte Orions. This move extended his playing career for another four seasons. He was one of the first big-name former Major Leaguers to play in Japan and in 1974 became the first professional baseball player to win a championship title in both the United States and Japan. During this time, I think my parents tried to keep their marriage together. It was a futile effort. I'm guessing they would have split much sooner if it hadn't been for me.

I really don't know all the details of what went wrong with my parents' marriage. Maybe they didn't have the necessities in common and shouldn't have married in the first place.

But it's interesting to me now that when I was a teenager, it always seemed to me that my Mom suffered far more over the divorce than my Dad. I'm not so sure of that anymore. What I've figured out since is that they both suffered. They just handled it differently.

I could sense my Mom's anger toward my Dad all the time. She coped with this anger by essentially transforming herself into someone else – a party girl. I don't recall sensing my Dad's pain back then, but now as I've become a little more educated in human behavior, I believe the pain was there, just like my Mom's. While my Mom may have tried to dull her pain with chemicals, my Dad may have tried to bury his in baseball. Human beings are naturally wired to seek pleasure and avoid pain. Dealing with my Mom and the divorce must have been painful for him. He immersed himself in baseball. His playing career behind him, he began to read every book he could about the game. He published a book with his father,

The *Making of a Hitter*. He and his brother started a baseball equipment company, Lefebvre Training Aids, which included the first batting tee. He used his name and influence to get to know some of the most accomplished coaches in this country as a means of figuring out new ways to inspire players. And he could inspire. He was energetic and charismatic. Players enjoyed working with him. Baseball general managers wanted to hire him. Companies wanted him to endorse their products. He always had a solution for his professional life. But, like his oldest son discovered in the summer of 2005, his personal life was another matter.

Although we haven't ever talked in depth about what I lived through in 2005, I believe there is an unspoken understanding between us now. He wasn't a perfect father. I wasn't a perfect son. We have two options to choose from now. We can either dwell in the past about what could have been or should have been, or we can love each other. That has worked quite well for us.

Lunch With Robert

I managed to make it through the Gloves for Kids event after my therapy meeting with Dale. I wasn't too concerned about having an emotional breakdown at the Gloves for Kids event because I felt drained after leaving Dale's office. I went home that night, mentally exhausted, and actually seemed to catch a few uninterrupted hours of sleep. The next day, August 9, I awoke, cautious of how I was going to feel. But I had something to look forward to: I was going to have lunch with one of my most precious friends, Robert Rogers. He is, quite simply, one of the most amazing people I know. We met at a banquet in the fall of 2004.

If you don't know his story, it goes like this:

On the night of August 30, 2003, Robert and his family were returning from Wichita, Kansas, where they had attended a wedding, to their home in Liberty, Missouri (just north of Kansas City). While traveling north on Interstate 35, their car suddenly came upon a flash flood that had overtaken the highway and engulfed it in 4-foot-high, raging waters. Robert's wife, Melissa, was driving while Robert sat in the passenger's seat and their four children were in back. Melissa attempted to drive through the flooding waters by following a semi-truck. But their minivan stalled, and the family became trapped inside, unable to open the electric windows. The waters shook and tossed the minivan about, as Melissa and Robert tried to devise a plan of escape for their family. Robert eventually kicked out a door window and was sucked through the opening and far away from the minivan. Robert eventually found his way to dry land. But Melissa, and their daughter, Makenah, weren't so fortunate in the rapids. They were found the next morning, drowned, almost a mile from the minivan. The three other children were also found drowned the next morning in the overturned van. In an instant, a family of six had been reduced to one.

Robert lived in the same house in Liberty for years

but naturally his life changed dramatically. Soon after the tragedy, he quit his job as an electrical engineer and devoted his life to sharing his story, and to his ministry Living Life with No Regrets. He believes, even through the horrific events of that night, that he was somehow touched by God on that fateful evening.

Normally, our lunch get-togethers and conversations had nothing to do with my anxieties or worries. But on this day, Robert wound up spending most of the time trying to lift my spirits. I have often thought how bizarre this must have seemed to him. This was less than two years following the death of his wife and four children, and yet, here he was, trying to restore my hope. But that's the type of person Robert is. His warmth and compassion are unequaled. As I explained to Robert all the things that were going on in my mind, he sat quietly and nodded. He seemed to understand. There was a peace within him that simply awed me. I have to admit, I yearned for that peace. He explained to me that while my crisis might not theoretically compare to his crisis, it didn't really matter. His pain had been real. His pain was real. So was my pain. He said I needed to acknowledge my pain, to meet it head-on, and to own it. I wasn't entirely sure what he meant, but he said it so confidently, so commandingly, I think I actually felt some of his peace right at that moment. I know that sounds strange.

New York

My "condition" took a turn for the worse on August 27, 2005. I had been going to therapy for almost three weeks, and while I was still experiencing some mild anxiety, I was feeling better. Thanks to Dale helping bring to light what was at the core of my issues – a sense of abandonment – I actually had felt a greater sense of calm. Even though I was far from "healed," I was getting a clearer picture of what was ailing me. In my mind, I was getting a little better.

The Royals were in New York City for a weekend series with the Yankees starting August 26. I'm not a huge fan of New York but I've grown to abide the city a little more each year. I always used to say that the highlight of any trip to The Big Apple was when the captain says, "Flight attendants, please prepare for departure." I always felt intimidated by the crowds and the noise of the city. Visiting teams stay in midtown, a place I used to have one thing in common with – it never slept, either. There are people and car horns everywhere. It doesn't take long to hear a jackhammer in this part of the city because midtown is always under construction. Yet as time has gone by, I have learned to appreciate the energy of New York City for what it is and I have tried to take in all that this unique city has to offer.

We didn't get to our hotel until about 4 AM on August 26, due to a late game in Kansas City against Boston the evening prior. Late-night-early-morning flights are one of the less glamorous parts of the job and thankfully it doesn't happen too often. After getting some sleep that morning, I decided to take a short walk to a nearby deli for lunch. I started to feel even more uncomfortable than usual as I walked around midtown near the team hotel. It just seemed more crowded and noisy than I remembered. I recall feeling very uneasy and decided to take my sandwich back to the room rather than eat at the deli. I wasn't very concerned at the time about any type of emotional breakdown or anxiety relapse. I just figured I was still tired from the early morning arrival and needed to get a nap before heading to Yankee Stadium. The nap helped but I never felt comfortable that night. Broadcasting the game helped take my mind off my uneasiness for a few hours, but I could feel myself slipping emotionally on the bus ride back to the hotel. I had some difficulty falling asleep that night but I thought perhaps it was simply because I was overtired.

Sunlight burst through the drapes in my hotel room

Something is wrong with me. I'm not happy. Why am I not happy? I'm never happy. Who would want to be with me? I'm going to be alone the rest of my life.

on the morning of August 27. The start of a beautiful day? Hardly. I experienced one of the trademarks of depression that morning; I didn't want to get out of bed. I awoke almost two hours before my 7 AM alarm and I immediately felt like something devastating had happened to me. But as I quickly took inventory, I realized that nothing devastating had happened to me the night before. Still, it felt like I had been delivered some awful news, like my best friend had died, or a family member had been diagnosed with cancer, or something dreadful like that. My mind was once again playing tricks with me. Dale and others had warned me about the lies that fill your head when depression sets in. The lies started in again: Something is wrong with me. I'm not happy. Why am I not happy? I'm never happy. Who would want to be with me? I'm going to be alone the rest of my life. I felt myself slipping into the darkness again.

One of the Royals players, Mike Sweeney, had planned a night on the town following the game that afternoon. We were going to have dinner with his agent,

Seth Levinson, and John Buck, another Royals player whom Seth represented. Yet all I could think about that morning was staying in bed. If I was somehow able to get out of bed and broadcast the game, I needed to find an excuse to get out of dinner and the Broadway show Mike had planned for us to attend. There was no way I could get through the game and a night out. I knew I couldn't keep it together that long.

I finally forced myself to get out of bed, shower, and dress. I knew I had just enough time to get on my lap-top computer and go through my usual pre-game preparation of gathering notes and anecdotes on the players. But within a minute or two it became obvious that I simply couldn't concentrate. I was completely incapable of focusing long enough to surf and read through the daily baseball websites I had visited every day of my Major League broadcasting career. For the first time in 11 seasons, I didn't prepare for a game. I simply couldn't do it. And I didn't care. I was on radio that day and the saving grace was that we were going to have a three-man booth. All I had to do was get through six of the nine innings (former Royals broadcaster Fred White would do the other three innings) and try to get former Royal Brian McRae to do most of the talking. If I could pull this off, I rationalized, I didn't need to prepare. For anyone who knows me during the baseball season, my three biggest priorities are: My routine, my routine, and my routine. I have it down to an actual minute-by-minute science from waking up, having breakfast, doing my pre-game preparation, working out, having lunch, taking a nap, taking a shower, and going to the ballpark. My routine is almost religious to me. Not on this day, however.

Normally, the bus ride to Yankee Stadium makes a strong impression on me. Traveling from midtown to the Bronx allows for some of the best people-watching in America. The frantic pace of life in New York quite often makes me feel better about the laid-back pace of life on little ol' Lake Winnebago back in Missouri. The trip from midtown to the Bronx can also make you sad and reflective. Back in 2005, right before the bus pulled up to old Yankee Stadium, you'd pass a detention center (since demolished). It was common to see a young woman across the street from the detention center holding her child up in the air just so the child's father could see. I can remember on a past trip seeing one mother trying to point to a particular hand sticking out of an iron-barred window as if to say to her baby, "See, there's Daddy." It's sad. Images like that stick with me.

But on this day, August 27, I didn't look out the

window of the bus very much. I spent most of the time on the phone with my Mom. I explained to her that I was slipping again and tried to offer a few explanations. She tried to comfort me by saying it was late in the season and that normally I'm pretty worn out by the end of August. I just needed more sleep, she said. Easier said than done.

The team bus pulled up to Yankee Stadium at about 10:30 that morning. I remember taking deep breaths as I entered the stadium. While unpacking my bag in the visitor's radio booth, I noticed one of our players had his son on the field. I took out my binoculars and saw that it was Joe McEwing with his son, Joseph. I sat down in my chair and just watched a father and his son enjoy a special moment together before the stadium gates opened. I'm sure Joseph will never remember that day but Joe looked so proud. I thought about my own Dad.

Although I had never met him before 2005, Joe McEwing had become one of my favorite players to work with during my career. He wasn't the most gifted player on the field, but he knew how to play, how to accept his role, how to motivate and keep his teammates accountable, and (most importantly) how to interact with a certain 34-year-old play-by-play announcer. I concluded very early on in our friendship that Joe McEwing was a good man, as good as it gets. He had a beautiful son, a beautiful wife, and another baby on the way. As I watched Joe and his son on the field, something just screamed inside of me, "This is what happens to good men." Predictably, my mind started working its dark magic again, turning Joe's special moment with Joseph into a reminder of how alone I was: Joe deserved his life because he was a good man. I didn't deserve it because I wasn't a good man. I was also ungrateful for the things I had. There are people with real tragedy and hardship out there and they somehow manage to get by without getting depressed. Not me. I cry, just like I'm doing now, filling up these binoculars with tears. What is wrong with me? I am losing my mind.

That's the way anxiety grinds at you. Destructive thoughts fuel the depression. It is an indescribably helpless feeling. I was lost. But as I sat the binoculars down, I knew I had to somehow pull it together. I was about to tape my weekly interview with Royals general manager Allard Baird in about 30 minutes. After letting the tears dry, I grabbed my recorder and headed for the field, all the way thinking of excuses to bow out of the evening Michael Sweeney had planned for us.

As I entered the visitor's clubhouse, the best I could come up with for an excuse was that I was worn down from the late arrival two nights before and wasn't feeling good. Michael would understand, I figured. Plus, he could invite any one of his teammates. Michael's locker at Yankee Stadium was on the opposite side of the room from the entrance. It's not a big room but it seemed big on this day. As I approached his locker I noticed he wasn't there. I was upset and relieved at the same time. Upset that I didn't get to back out and relieved that he wasn't there because I know he would have asked me how I was doing. This would have led to who knows how many tears and I didn't want that to happen in front of a room full of Major League Baseball players. As I turned to head back for the entrance I heard, "Hey Ryno!" There was Michael, coming out of the players' lounge, with his traditional smile. "Hey bud, I am so fired up for tonight. You are going to love this restaurant. I'm not kidding – it might be my favorite in the league."

Anyone who knows Michael knows about his genuine enthusiasm for life. Even the most hard-shelled sportswriters and sportscasters around the league have a soft spot for Michael because they sense that in a sport filled with selfish and superficial stars, he is the real deal. He is sincere. You just have to see it and feel it. It was that sincerity that made me forget my plan to beg off dinner and the show. I agreed with our post-game plans and

When depression binds up your soul, everyone else's life seems so much more appealing than your own.

was on my way. But as I walked away, I thought, “How in the world am I going to get through it?”

As I left the clubhouse and stepped down into the visitor’s dugout at Yankee Stadium, Joe and Joseph were still playing on the field. After Joe and I exchanged a couple of pleasantries, Joe handed his son to his wife, Julia, kissed her and Joseph goodbye, and bounded into the dugout and back up the tunnel for the clubhouse. Life looked so beautiful for the McEwings and so dark and ugly for me. I know now and I knew then that there are no perfect situations in life. There are no perfect jobs, marriages, or children. Yet when depression binds up your soul, everyone else’s life seems so much more appealing than your own.

A crowd of 54,452 fans jammed into Yankee Stadium to watch the hometown team score five runs in the bottom of the ninth inning to beat the Royals, 8-7. Although I got through the broadcast, I don’t remember much about the game except dreading, once again, having to go out on the town afterward. Once all of my on-air responsibilities were complete, I waited for Michael at the entrance to the stadium.

I love Mike Sweeney like a brother. But being his friend means being flexible with regard to being on time. After pacing in front of the stadium for an eternity (10 minutes), I decided to go back into the stadium and walk off some of my anxiety. I was starting to sweat and I could feel my heart begin to pound. As I reentered the ballpark, I ran into a number of Royals' wives who had made the trip to New York. This was just what I needed; a reminder that a bunch of our players were going to have their loved ones waiting for them to enjoy Manhattan. Again, a reminder of how alone I was. I actually ran into Michael's cousins from New Jersey. A few years back they had visited Kansas City and spent the day at my house and on the lake. I managed to be polite and kept the conversation light. Next, I had a conversation with Larisa Affeldt, the wife of relief pitcher Jeremy Affeldt. Truth be told, Jeremy blew the game that afternoon at Yankee Stadium with a terrible outing in the ninth. Larisa and Jeremy had planned their own night on the town in New York City but I could tell she was wondering how much Jeremy would be in the mood to follow through with the plan. I remember thinking I would gladly trade my pain for the pain Jeremy went through that day – the humiliation he faced in front of his teammates and the more than 54,000 delighted Yankee fans after blowing a big lead. At least Jeremy had someone to spend the rest of the night with who cared about him and his bad day. I had no one that understood my agony. Michael finally called and said he was on his way out. Thank God, because I felt that there was no way I could make it another minute. When Michael finally arrived he put his arm around me and again declared, "Ryno, you're going to love this place. I'm starving. Wait until you try the Chilean sea bass. It just melts in your mouth."

Here I had a glimmer of hope. Maybe I was hungry. Maybe my blood-sugar was low. I really don't know what that means but perhaps it applied to me and perhaps a meal might snap me out of this deep funk. Michael, Seth, and John talked all the way to the restaurant. I just stayed quiet, trying to prevent myself from going insane.

We arrived at the trendy Asian restaurant, Tao, but only had about an hour to eat before we had to get in a cab and head to the show "The Producers." The food was incredible but the atmosphere wasn't what I needed. Tao is stylish but dimly lit with rather loud music. I immediately felt uncomfortable. Five minutes after taking our seats I was in big trouble. I tried to make conversation to distract my own thinking but the world was slowly caving in on me. I began to sweat while the others complained about how cold it was. I had my hands folded in my lap in between bites, squeezing as hard as I could. Both of my legs were in a constant twitch. I could feel my heart pounding. There was a warm and tingling sensation in the center of my chest as if I had been injected with some sort of burning fluid. It started to spread slowly to my shoulders and down toward my stomach. I was going to pass out at any moment. Everywhere I looked, people were laughing and smiling and having a wonderful time. What was happening to me? Isn't there one other person in this place that's feeling what I'm feeling? I did notice that just about everyone inside the restaurant was enjoying an alcoholic beverage. I had been sober for seven-and-a-half years, but truly felt like I needed a drink right that minute. It was undoubtedly the strongest urge I had felt for a drink since late January of 1998. I needed to medicate myself somehow before I caused a scene. But Michael knew of my sobriety and the problems I had experienced before coming to Kansas City in 1999. So ordering a drink to prevent a scene might have caused an even bigger scene.

I don't know how it feels right before you have a heart attack, a stroke, or a seizure, but I felt like something horrible was about to happen. I kept thinking, though, that the last thing I wanted to do was disappoint or embarrass Michael in a public place. Michael was a great friend. I was about to ruin this night on the town he had been anticipating for weeks. My heart was pounding so hard I was sure it was going to explode at any moment. The room appeared to become smaller and louder with every heartbeat. I could feel the sweat continue to build. It was starting to run down my face. As Michael talked I pictured him the next day at the ballpark answering questions from reporters about my incident. Meanwhile, if I survived, I pictured myself in some New York City hospital in a straight jacket hoping for a transfer back to Kansas City. That's what was going through my mind when Michael turned to me and said, "Ryno, you have to check out the bathrooms here. They are awesome."

God speaks to us in many ways. As ridiculous as this sounds, I believe this was God using Michael to save me in some way. I decided at that exact moment it was a perfect time to check out Tao's bathrooms. I immediately got up and walked to the back of the restaurant, down some stairs (I think) and into a truly unique potty experience. You actually peed into a wall-mounted waterfall. I headed straight for the sinks. I looked at myself in the mirror thinking I was going to see something gray or green staring back at me but was amazed to discover I looked somewhat normal for a 34-year-old, huge foreheaded, blue-eyed male. I started splashing cold water on my face as they do in the movies. You know, right before the lawyer goes back into the courtroom before making his closing remarks in a totally unwinnable case? If it worked for him, maybe it would work for me.

After about 10 minutes in the waterfall restroom, I returned to the table feeling slightly better. We still had about 20 minutes before Michael and I had to leave for the show. Every minute was an eternity but we finally got up from the table and I couldn't wait to get outside. Something told me I might survive this evening if I could just get some fresh air. We hailed a cab and were on our way to the show. Michael knew something was wrong with me and asked if I was feeling OK. I told him I had some things on my mind and I was tired. He knew I wasn't telling the truth but quickly changed the subject to "The Producers." He was very excited to see the show that all of his friends said was the best they had ever seen. We arrived at the theater just as the curtain opened and sat down about four rows from the stage. Any other night I would have been pretty impressed with such a close-up view of the stage and actors, but not that night. It was far too close for a person about to snap and lose his mind. Five minutes into the show, I was ready for it to be over. There were a few moments that caused me to laugh but, for the most part, it was forced. Michael kept looking at me during humorous scenes to see how I was reacting. By this time he was well aware that I was troubled.

When we reached the intermission, we left our seats for the restroom. I was happy just to get up and move around. However, the line was long and moved slowly. I couldn't make eye contact with Michael because I knew he would see the misery all over my face. Finally he put his arm around me and said, "What's going on? You want to talk about it?" That was more than I could take. Tears started rolling down my cheeks. I just shook my head as if to say I wasn't able to talk about it. He just kept his arm around me and rubbed my shoulders like a father would for his recently "cut-from-the-team" son.

We got through the show and headed back to the hotel. On the way, Michael asked, "What is it?" I shook my head and said, "I don't know. It feels like a lot of things." I suggested we talk after we got back to our rooms. I couldn't begin in the cab because I didn't know where to start. I just wanted to get back to the privacy of my room and call my Mom.

Thankfully I didn't see anyone from our traveling party in the hotel lobby. The moment I got inside my room, I fell to my bed and absolutely lost it. I was frightened. It was as if I realized I was lost in another country, far from home. I felt completely disconnected from the world. I didn't know anyone and nobody understood me. I cried as hard as is humanly possible. I was certain that I needed to be hospitalized. After several minutes I called my Mom in Albuquerque. Thankfully she answered.

"Hi, Honey, how's New York?"

Through sobs, I said, "Not good."

"What's wrong?"

Overwhelmed with emotion, I couldn't respond.

"Honey, are you OK? Tell me what happened?"

"I don't know. I'm just so sad. I don't know what's wrong with me."

"Did anything happen today that made you feel this way?"

"I don't know. I just wish you were here."

With that my Mom decided she would meet me in Kansas City when I got home from New York. Having suffered through her own depressive episodes, she always worried that I would eventually meet that fate, too. She told me we would go see a doctor together and that she would stay with me in KC as long as I needed her. She also assured me that I was going to be fine. All I had to do was get through one more day and I would be on my way home. She did most of the talking because I couldn't speak. Slowly, her words calmed me down as she recounted her experiences of feeling severely depressed. After about 45 minutes I ran out of tears and she relaxed me to a point where we could have some semblance of a conversation. I asked her if she felt some of the things I was feeling. Whether she meant it or not, she said yes. I could sense that she was hurting for me but she instinctively started doing her motherly magic. She persuaded me to take a hot shower, drink some cold water, get into bed, and call her back.

Following her orders, I called her back at 12:30 AM, tucked into bed. At this point I was exhausted. I told Mom I was feeling a little better and promised to call her first thing in the morning. I hung up the phone, turned off the light, and started to fall asleep thinking the worst was over. It was not.

The worst part ended up being the best part for me. I fell asleep in less than three minutes but woke up at 2:30 AM in a pool of sweat. This was a new deal. I had been waking up early in the weeks leading up to this night, but never like this. I rolled over to see the clock and was stunned that I had only slept for two hours. I could feel a warm, tight sensation in my chest. I was having trouble taking the deep breaths I used during the past couple of weeks to try to calm myself down. My heart was pounding. I noticed I was clenching my teeth.

This was different from what I was experiencing at Tao but equally as frightening. I did the best I could to try to ignore it all and fall back asleep but I had the energy to run a marathon. There was no chance I was going to go back to sleep anytime soon. I got up and thought about calling the front desk to see if there was a hospital close by. As I contemplated this I splashed some more cold water on my face to try to cool myself down. I needed to talk to someone but everyone was going to be asleep at this hour. I got back into bed and stared at the ceiling, trying to figure out what was causing all of this. When I couldn't come up with a logical solution, I realized I needed some help. Maybe I had a "chemical imbalance" that Mom always talked about when describing her condition years before. Maybe all of this had very little to do with my emotions and perhaps some medication would get me back on track. The mind is amazingly powerful and when I started to see this pain from a different light, I started to calm down. I stared at the ceiling for about an hour, fantasizing a doctor giving me some medication and me feeling like my old self. This also calmed me and I fell back asleep for a few more hours.

The next morning on the way to Yankee Stadium I told Fred White what had happened the night before and what had been going on the past few weeks. He was the first person with the Royals that I shared this information with. He spent the entire subway trip to

I stared at the ceiling for about an hour, fantasizing a doctor giving me some medication and me feeling like my old self.

the Bronx telling me the team would support me in any way it could, that I was free to take some time off if I needed, and that I needed to remind myself of how many friends I had that would support me if I allowed them to do so. I consider Fred White a great friend. He was right there to lend support. What an unlikely father figure he had become in seven years. Fired after 25 years as a full-time Royals announcer, he was replaced by me. The city was in an uproar but nobody supported me more than Fred White. Now he was lending me his friendship and support through the darkest days of my life. His words that morning helped put my mind at ease as we pulled up to the subway station at Yankee Stadium.

I was able to get through the television broadcast that afternoon but felt jittery. I remember almost jumping out of my skin a few times when I heard a door close, or a named yelled. I guess you could have diagnosed me as in "serious but stable condition."

Fred White

I was a young announcer for the Minnesota Twins when I heard about Fred White being fired by the Royals. It was at the end of the 1998 season. I had an agent at the time and she called to ask if I might be interested in the Royals radio job. My answer came without delay, "Heck no. I'm not going to be the idiot that tries to replace Fred White." There's an old rule that broadcasters follow when it comes to taking a new job: Don't replace the legend, replace the guy who replaced the legend. In other words, if at all possible don't put yourself in the position of being the strange, new voice after a longtime, popular announcer has departed (for whatever reason). I experienced some of this in Minnesota. In my second season with the Twins in 1996, Herb Carneal stopped doing the majority of road games and I became his replacement on radio. I was thrilled to be a TV and radio announcer for a big league team at the age of 25. The Twins seemed equally excited and were wonderful about promoting me before the 1996 season began. However, a large portion of the listening audience was not so thrilled. They had been listening to Herb for 34 seasons and had grown to love his voice calling baseball. Even though I had been a three-time all-Big Ten outfielder for the University of Minnesota, had a father that played, coached, and managed in the Major Leagues, and had been warmly greeted as part of the TV team, I wasn't received well by the regular radio audience. They wanted Herb. It took Twins radio fans quite some time to warm up to me. So, after having gone through that, I had no intention of going to a new city where I had no roots and where fans had no idea who I was. Plus, Fred had been fired, which angered Royals fans. I would just be some 28-year-old kid from Minnesota who was replacing the lovable Fred White.

"Are you sure you're not interested?" my agent asked.

"I'm positive!" I said.

A couple of months later, I was having difficulty negotiating my 1999 radio contract in Minnesota when KMBZ, the Royals radio rights holder, called me directly about the radio position. I still had no interest in the

Royals job but saw an opportunity to gain some leverage with WCCO radio in Minneapolis by looking into the Royals position. I accepted an interview and flew to Kansas City in December of 1998. A writer at the *Minneapolis Star-Tribune*, Lavelle Neal, caught wind of my trip to KC. He had written for the *Kansas City Star* before moving to Minneapolis. I remember sitting in a first class seat on Northwest Airlines to Kansas City and reading a headline in the *Star-Tribune*, Lefebvre to Interview with Royals. This was perfect! WCCO was really going to panic now. At this point, the Kansas City job was still just a negotiating tool. My heart was in Minneapolis. Well, that all changed about three minutes after walking off the plane in KC when KMBZ program director Bill White informed me that I was their number one candidate and that they would pay me more money to do Royals games than I was making in Minnesota doing the Twins and the University of Minnesota on radio and TV. I could do whatever I wanted during the baseball off-season. Bill had listened to my tape and detailed why they were so interested in my work. We drove to Kauffman Stadium and had lunch in the Stadium Club where Vice President of Marketing Mike Levy and General Manager Herk Robinson praised me and hoped I would strongly consider the position. All of a sudden, I'm remembering how much I loved Kauffman Stadium and eating Gates barbecue. I began to see an opportunity to gain more radio experience and prove that I could handle a 162-game schedule. I saw an opportunity to make a name for myself without any add-ons to my name like: Ryan Lefebvre, son of Jim Lefebvre.

I never had another meeting with WCCO radio in Minnesota. I wanted the Royals job. I knew I was making the right decision but I had the typical buyer's remorse after doing so. I knew it wasn't going to be easy replacing Fred. I actually accepted the job on December 23 while I was visiting my grandparents in Wisconsin for

Christmas. To celebrate my decision, I took my grandmother and grandfather out for dinner. As soon as we walked into The Coral Reef in tiny Rochester, Wisconsin, the Dinner Special marquee caught my eye. The special that night was the Kansas City Strip. I thought that was a good sign.

Three years earlier, I had poked my head in the Royals radio booth during a Royals-Twins series at the Metrodome and met Fred. I wanted to listen to Fred and Denny Matthews' broadcast of the game simply to learn. Fred introduced himself back then with a big smile and encouraged me to stick around. That left

Denny Matthews, me, and Fred White

such an impression on me. I hadn't forgotten his kindness back then so I decided to call him and tell him that I accepted the job he had held for 25 years. I was quite uneasy about what to say but I knew I owed him a call. In typical Fred White fashion, he was as gracious as ever. "Ryan, all I can tell you is that you have accepted a great job. I wish you the best and I'll be happy to help you in any way that I can." That took a huge load off my back.

I had done only about two spring training games for the Royals in 1999 when the complaints about the "new guy" started to file in. A Kansas City sports radio show was in Florida to cover the Royals' first week

> The first two years in Kansas City were rough. I received some nasty e-mail and letters, was regularly mocked by a local talk show host, and felt like listeners were waiting for me to make a mistake.

of exhibition games. Fred had taken a position with Metro Sports, a Kansas City all-sports cable television station, and was also in Florida. The radio station asked Fred to come on as a guest to talk about the Royals. The calls started to pour in. Royals' fans wanted Fred back and the new guy out. It was one call after another. After taking several calls, Fred did something I will never forget and something he didn't have to do. He basically said, "Look, I'm thankful that all of you appreciate me and wish I was still calling the games. But Ryan Lefebvre is a good announcer and a good guy. His voice isn't familiar now but I really think you need to give him a chance. Give him a fair opportunity to show you what he can do. He had nothing to do with my firing. Just give him a chance." Now that's a man with character.

The first two years in Kansas City were rough. The Royals and KMBZ mostly supported me but the team wasn't playing well and Denny Matthews and I were delivering mostly bad news each night. I received some nasty e-mail and letters, was regularly mocked by a local talk show host, and felt like listeners were waiting for me to make a mistake. Through it all, though, Fred was supportive and encouraging. Then things changed during my third season. Denny began to cut back on his road schedule, missing about 15-20 games a year. The man hired to replace him? Fred White. Even though Fred and I got along off the air and Fred publicly supported me, nobody had heard the two of us together. We really hit it off as broadcast partners. We talked about the game, laughed, and had a good time. All of a sudden it was as if the listeners said to themselves, "If Fred says he's OK, then maybe he is OK." I'm not saying every Royals radio listener fell in love with me overnight but I felt much more accepted after working with Fred during that 2001 season.

Several people admitted that they noticed something different about me in 2005. I wasn't as outgoing and engaging as I normally was, and I would disappear for long periods of time. Fred wasn't uncomfortable asking me if I was OK on that late August morning in 2005. From that day on, Fred was always making sure I was getting along all right and that I was aware of the team's support. He would call me at home and on the road in my hotel room to check in with me. He would stop by the booth at home and suggest we eat together on the road. When I felt overwhelmed at the stadium, I would stop by his office for a closed-door heart-to-heart chat. Fred White was like a guardian angel that I could talk to, all the while reminding me of how many friends I had that cared about me and that the Royals would support me in any way they could.

Not Alone

Getting back home from New York helped, but knowing my Mom was on her way from New Mexico really relieved my anxiety. Before she arrived I had an important discussion with an old friend who was still in baseball and who was in town for the series against the Royals. After our game on Monday night, August 29, my friend asked me how I was doing. After sharing my story with Fred the day before in New York, I was more comfortable opening up to someone else in baseball. I didn't hesitate being completely honest with my friend. How he responded, however, took me by surprise: "You know, I haven't told many people this, but..."

He explained that in 1991 he had had a similar experience. We exchanged stories about how our minds tried to trick us into believing things that didn't exist, and how we thought the condition made us feel as though we were losing our minds. Just hearing that someone else, let alone a close friend, had shared a similar experience, was an injection of hope. My friend then had a very confident and reassuring look on his face as he said, "Feev, you will get better. Once I got on the proper medication…no more."

I wanted to know how long it took for the medication to kick in. He said that he started to notice a difference after two weeks, and after two months he never had a bad attack again. He stayed on the medication for about a year, slowly weaned himself off, and never needed it again, he said. Man, that was music to my ears. Again, he assured me I was going to be fine.

Mom arrived on Tuesday, August 30, and I had a doctor's appointment set for that Thursday. I was feeling pretty good: I was home, my friend had encouraged me because of his recovery from a similar condition, Mom was in town, and I was about to see a doctor about medication that would make this entire bad dream go away. I was feeling comfort I hadn't experienced in three weeks.

When I talked to my doctor, Ronald Nichol, about my condition, he asked a few follow-up questions. He never looked alarmed. I don't know what Dr. Nichol is like away from his office, but he's about as cool as it comes in his white laboratory coat in an examination room. Even though I knew I wasn't the first person in the history of modern medicine to be hit with something like this, I still imagined that my doctor would appear to be somewhat alarmed. Maybe I had just grown accustomed to everyone else's surprise when I told them how bad I was feeling. Dr. Nichol then explained that what I was experiencing was fairly common and that he was going to give me a couple of medications. I was going on the daily anti-depressant Lexapro to help stabilize my overall condition. I also would have some low doses of Xanex in the event of an anxiety/panic attack. I asked Dr. Nichol how long I would have to wait to feel better. He said the Lexapro would take at least two weeks and possibly as long as two months. At that very moment I realized that the word week was a much more beautiful-sounding word than the word month. He also explained that most people level out around one month but cautioned me that everyone is different. Dr. Nichol also explained that the Xanex would be used on an as-needed basis and that its effects were pretty rapid. He handed me the prescriptions, asked me to schedule an appointment for a month later, and that was it. Again, I was surprised yet pleased to see how nonchalant he was.

Mom told me that during her first bout with depression the medication didn't kick in for about six weeks. When she quit the medication and had a subsequent relapse, it took five months for her to feel right again. So I knew I wouldn't be cured when I popped my first 10mg of Lexapro on September 1, 2005, but at least I was on my way to recovery. This gave me an immediate sense of calm. I took my regular pre-game nap that afternoon and awoke calm and refreshed rather than sweaty and anxious. One half-day into my medication and I felt a tiny sense of control. There is no way the medication was working yet but that little white pill put my mind at ease. I learned quite a bit about the power of the mind during this ordeal.

Having Mom in Kansas City gave me someone to talk to during my usual alone times prior to and after the games. As is the case with most people suffering from depression and anxiety, psychotherapy is a wonderful tool for recovery. Just talking about what was bouncing around my mind and getting it out instead of storing it and fighting it provided a release. Being alone and hemmed in by your thoughts is fuel for depression.

Mom was wonderful at identifying my bad moments or even when a bad moment was starting to build. She recognized a certain look in my eyes and would say, "What are you thinking right now?" She must have asked me that five times a day. No matter how ridiculous the thoughts were, I shared them with her, every last detail. Having been through this awful experience herself, she remembered thinking a lot of the same thoughts. Having recovered from two bouts, she knew how irrational one can get. So as soon as I would say something like, "I've forgotten what makes me happy," Mom would quickly respond, "That's normal, Ryan. I felt the same way. This will pass and you will remember what makes you happy again. I promise." She wouldn't allow me to fall victim to the lies while I was in her presence.

I'd say, "I'm going to live in this big, lonely house the rest of my life."

"You're worrying about the future just like I did. When you get better – and you will get better – are you listening to me? You will get better. Look at me! You will get better – and when you get better you won't worry about the future like you are now. You will get back to enjoying each day as it comes and you will fill this house with a great, big family."

That's what my Mom did for me for six days. She was my rock.

I didn't have to use the Xanex until September 4, the day my Mom left. I wanted her to stay the rest of the season. I didn't want her to leave, but she needed to get back to her life in New Mexico, and I needed to find a way to make it alone. I didn't want her to feel guilty about leaving on that Sunday morning, so it took quite a bit of strength for me to hold it together on the drive to the airport. After I dropped her off, I popped my first Xanex because I could feel the monster building inside of me. Again, there was a sense of calm immediately after taking the pill as my mind knew relief was coming. This alone made me feel better.

I drove to the stadium for an afternoon game with the Texas Rangers and had to pop another pill before the game. For about two innings, I felt like I was going to fall asleep. I was trying to call the game and prevent myself from nodding off at the same time. (Now I know what it's like listening to me on the radio.) I decided to call one of the innings standing up just to stay alert and to keep my blood flowing. Fortunately, I got through the game. I wouldn't need Xanex for another six days.

Alcohol

By most accounts I was a shy but polite young boy. I think the shy part was my nature and the polite part was what my mother demanded. We moved several times during my school days. Between first grade and twelfth grade we lived in four different houses, and I attended six schools. I hated being the new kid in town. I got along with most kids in school but was always pretty shy around girls, especially the ones I felt a physical attraction toward. I always admired boys who had no problem talking to girls.

At the age of 14, I got drunk for the first time and I became extremely sick. Yet a funny thing happened on the way to the toilet: I loved the feeling of being drunk.

I was pretty bashful when it came to approaching the opposite sex until high school. Luckily for me, and I don't know what it was like elsewhere, but girls in Los Angeles seemed confident, at least confident in themselves enough to make the first move, like sending me a note saying, "Will you go out with me? Yes, no or maybe?"

During my freshman year of high school I met an influential friend who would be with me through the best of times and the worst of times for the next 12 years: alcohol. At the age of 14 in the fall of 1985, I got drunk for the first time and I became extremely sick. Yet a funny thing happened on the way to the toilet: I loved the feeling of being drunk.

Alcohol brought another side of me out of its shell. I became the life of the party. I was much more confident approaching a girl or calling her on the phone. Alcohol allowed me to become the confident, outgoing type of kid I always wanted to be. Ironically, after all those years of despising what my Mom and her friends used to become when they were drunk, I became dependent on alcohol myself. But it was great medication.

Alcohol provided some problems, too. There were automobile accidents, fights, and other juvenile acts that got me into plenty of trouble with my parents and the law. There were the countless things I didn't mean to say to people (mostly girls) when I was under the influence. There were the many hangovers after a hard night and the famous, "I will never do this to myself again" proclamation the next day. While I may have meant it each time I said it, I knew deep down I couldn't have the social life I wanted without my buddy.

Living in Brentwood and going to a prestigious, private high school meant I was surrounded by a lot of wealthy kids. Money does seem to grow on trees in those parts, and there was always enough of it around to party.

Although I fit in because of athletics and my willingness to party with the big boys, I was also at the lower end of the financial spectrum of my new group of friends. I was "one of them" in many ways, but I wasn't in other ways. I always had a slight fear that one day I would be exposed and deposed. This made my intoxicated persona even more important.

I survived high school and accepted a baseball scholarship to the University of Minnesota. Again, I was the new kid in town, but I had alcohol to ease the transition into my new environment. The intense partying continued in college but didn't prevent me from having a successful baseball and academic career.

The drinking became a problem in the winter of 1991 when I was arrested for public intoxication and disorderly conduct and spent the night locked up. I shot my mouth off to the wrong people in detox and got the tar kicked out of me there. I had been humbled. That was the first time I seriously quit drinking. The embarrassment of the incident gave me the conviction to remain sober, and I wasn't tempted then to return to my former lifestyle. I had my first serious college girlfriend and was spending more time with her than with the boys. I also had the worst season of my college baseball career. I wasn't the same guy. I felt as though I was making good decisions, but those feelings of shyness and loneliness returned. I often felt depressed. After proving to myself that I could handle being sober for close to a year and feeling as if I had learned a valuable lesson, I started drinking again the next season. I was the life of the party again. I also had the best season of my college career. I was back.

After college, it didn't take long for me to have some success in broadcasting. But I missed playing baseball. I also missed the college scene and being one of the big men on campus. Now I was moving into an environment with older, more mature, more successful people. Alcohol still played a big role in helping me feel comfortable among new people. Two years into my full-time career, I was part of broadcast teams for the Minnesota Twins and the University of Minnesota hockey team. A lot of times, I didn't even have to buy my own alcohol. All I had to do now was show up at the right sports bar after a broadcast and there was always someone who wanted to buy me a drink and talk sports. In addition to my "on the air" responsibilities, I also adopted the added role of the wild, young TV "star" that all of the older members of the broadcast team lived vicariously through. Most of the others were married, so I provided the entertainment and the stories. Alcohol and I were still great partners.

But there were more instances of reckless behavior and so, in February of 1996, I decided I would quit drinking for the second time in my life. Just as in 1991, there was early momentum and determination after making such a decision. I stayed sober until October of 1997 when, just as in 1993, I decided I could handle alcohol again. There was no easing back into the alcohol and the party scene in 1997. I jumped right back in. I was at the height of my broadcasting career and I was out of control. Now I was letting everyone live vicariously through me. A talented, young radio and TV broadcaster one minute, I was an intoxicated, foul-mouthed, "nobody can mess with me" 26-year-old the next minute. I was becoming increasingly angry and violent when I was drunk. Friends warned me that I was going to throw my career and my life away. I was hanging around the wrong people and I was destroying myself. In a way, I sensed the damage I was doing. But I felt as though I had no other choice. I began to feel worse about my life when I wasn't intoxicated. I was surrounded by people, but I was alone and miserable. This meant that I needed even more alcohol to dig myself out of the emotional holes I was putting myself into.

On January 25, 1998, I made my final big mistake. After a fist fight on the University of Minnesota campus with a student, all of those words of warning began to sink in. It was the last time I took a drink. I was granted a leave of absence from my broadcasting job in Minnesota to get my life sorted out. I spent seven weeks of reflection and personal detoxification at my grandparents' house in rural Wisconsin. My grandparents were on their annual vacation to a warmer climate and I was all alone. At the time, the solitude was just what I needed. When those seven weeks were up, I felt refreshed and ready to re-enter the life I had started to create.

There was one problem: For twelve years I had used

alcohol to effectively medicate myself. Sobriety meant no more self-medication. My issues from childhood had always been present, ready to fill my mind with doubts and fears, but the alcohol had numbed them, too. Now, those doubts and fears weren't numb anymore. That's the part of sobriety most people aren't prepared for. There is plenty of praise for giving up your destructive lifestyle, but very little preparation for the ensuing pain. I'm not talking about the pain of addiction/withdrawal. I'm talking about all of the pain that alcohol helps temporarily divert. Alcohol never killed the pain; it just kept it far from the surface. On August 7, 2005, that pain finally reached the surface.

Detroit

After making it through the Texas game, with a lot of help from Xanex, we headed for a road trip through Chicago and Detroit. While in Chicago I was able to visit with my best friend, Eric Von Slagle. We have been best friends since our baseball playing days at the University of Minnesota. Like any great friend, Eric has seen me at my best and at my worst. Like any best friend, he is my biggest fan and has a knack for saying the right thing to pick me up off the floor when I need it. So I was looking for some comfort. But I was also looking forward to some education.

Eric works in the pharmaceutical industry. He began as a sales representative so he had to be well-informed about his product, at least informed enough to educate physicians about how his products worked. He told me that he would explain to me what might be wrong in terms of my chemical imbalance and how my prescribed drug, Lexapro, would help fix the problem.

He gave me a tutorial about how serotonin, dopamine, and norepinephrine work together in the brain and what each chemical controls. My trouble usually began with an obsession about the future which easily triggered anxiety, panic, and depression. So I had a problem with how serotonin was off-setting that trigger. The drug I

was taking was going to increase the amount of serotonin in my brain and give me a greater sense of calm. Eric and I had lunch in Chicago on September 8, exactly one week after I began using Lexapro. As he described how I would eventually feel, I explained to him that I was already feeling that way and that the drug had a surprisingly rapid effect on me. Then Eric dropped the hammer on me.

"Ry, the drug takes a month until it kicks in. You're just experiencing the placebo effect."

I didn't want to believe what he was saying. I truly did feel a great sense of peace.

He was adamant, "The mind is very powerful. It might be telling you that everything is fixed, but the drug takes at least a month until it starts working. Sometimes it takes longer."

I was not enjoying the sound of this at all. First it was a month, now it was at least a month. I thought I was on my way one week into the deal. On one hand I was upset that he rained on my parade with that information, but two days later I was extremely grateful he was so honest.

Saturday, September 10, started out a lot like the fateful weekend in New York had begun. We had arrived in Detroit from Chicago very late the night before and didn't get to the hotel until about 3 AM Friday, so I was pretty groggy most of that day. I was feeling a little anxious when I went to bed Friday evening, but didn't feel the need to take any Xanex for additional relief. At about 2 AM on Saturday I woke up with a racing heart. I was sweating like I had just walked out of a steam room. It wasn't as intense as the night in New York, but it was still bad. The warm and tingling sensations were there. Fortunately, now I had some defense. I popped a Xanex and was able to fall back asleep in less than an hour. I slept pretty soundly the rest of the night but was greeted by a deep, emotional aching on Saturday morning. The demons of doubt and fear apparently were waiting with a little depression breakfast-in-bed when I woke up at 7 AM. I literally couldn't motivate myself to get out of bed for close to four hours. I was exhausted, but I couldn't go back to sleep because the lies were screaming at me. I wondered if I would be physically or mentally capable of eating, showering, dressing, and going to the ballpark to announce a game. I honestly thought I was incapable of accomplishing any of these tasks, let alone the entire circuit. I thought of a few excuses I could use to get out of the game that night. In almost 11 full seasons in the Major Leagues I had never missed a game because of illness or any other reason. So if I told the Royals I couldn't go, I pretty much knew there wouldn't be any red flags. Perhaps if I just stayed in bed, popped a few more Xanex, and slept all day and night, I would be back in shape for the Sunday afternoon game. As I plotted my exit strategy, I realized that Eric was right. The medication had not kicked in yet. As upset as I was with the information on Thursday, I was very slightly relieved on this Saturday morning to know that I could still get better. If I hadn't had that conversation with him in Chicago, I might have really panicked in Detroit, already thinking I had been cured. This sliver of hope gave me enough motivation to call for room service. Maybe a $47 club sandwich at the Ritz Carlton would perk me up. At the very least, the bill would provide a little shock therapy.

The food did help enough to motivate me to take a shower. The shower motivated me to do my daily preparation. Once that was completed, I took a nap. Somewhat refreshed, I was able to get dressed and go to the ballpark.

Broadcasting baseball takes so much concentration that announcing a game does help take your mind off personal things for a few hours. In the summer of 2003, the games helped me get through a failed reconciliation with a former girlfriend. In 2005 however, I learned and felt the difference between feeling depressed and being depressed. In 2003 I felt depressed because I had some drama in my life, and announcing games was a way of clearing my mind. In 2005, I was suffering from Major Depressive Disorder. My mind was creating drama that didn't necessarily exist, and almost nothing was distracting enough to clear my mind. I was obsessed with my pain.

Somehow I got through the game on September 10, but it was agonizingly difficult. I don't know how well I described the game, but I was able to do so while focusing very clearly on keeping myself together as the medication slowly entered my system.

I returned to the hotel that night and called my Mom. I needed to talk to her because her voice and encouragement seemed the best medicine available at the time. Immediately she sensed by the tone of my voice that I was in trouble again. I'm sure she knew it wasn't going to be easy sailing for me when she left Kansas City the week before, but I know it hurt her to hear me sound the way I did. We fell right back into the routine we exercised while she was supporting me in KC.

"What's on your mind right now?" she asked.

"I don't know. I feel like everything is overwhelming me."

"That's completely normal, Honey. I felt the same way."

"It's only been a week. There's no way I'm going to be able to handle this pain for another three or four weeks."

"Yes you will. There will be moments like this but it gets better. I promise."

"I've never felt so alone in my life. I have all of these people around me that I've known for years but all of sudden I feel so detached from them."

"I remember feeling the same way. You feel like everyone else is doing great and nobody could possibly feel or understand the pain you're going through, right?"

The tears are flowing down my face at this point, "Yeah."

"Ryan, you have to listen to me. Your mind is playing tricks on you. You do know these people and they know you. They care about you and I know they would be willing to talk to you if you told them you needed a friend to listen."

"I don't want to do that to them."

"You're not doing anything to them. That's why they are your friends. I've met some of these people. They love you."

"I just want to stay in my room and talk to you."

"Then we'll talk as long as you need me."

Just like in New York, Mom told me to take a hot shower, drink some cold water, and call her back. I did and we talked until I was able to fall asleep. She got me through another dark day. I took more Xanex before going to sleep, and another after I woke up on Sunday. This Sunday was much like the one in New York two weeks before. We had an afternoon game and would be heading back to Kansas City. Just knowing I was going to get back home got me through September 11.

Therapy

My therapy sessions with Dale were always draining, almost like a physical workout. I always felt better afterward – it gave me a sense that I was at least doing something about my problem. What I really liked about Dale's approach is that during our sessions, she rarely wasted time on small talk. That suited me fine because I was eager to get better. I'd go into the office and within minutes, we were deep into discussion.

"So what exactly did you think all of this stuff was going to get you?" Dale asked.

"What stuff?" I said.

Dale looked down at her notes.

"Well, let's see," she said. "You wanted to be an announcer by a certain age, you wanted to make a certain salary, you wanted an impressive car and a big house.

What did you think this stuff was going to provide?"

"I guess I thought it would make me happy," I said, shrugging my shoulders.

"I'm sure you did but tell me what type of happy you were looking for?"

"A sense of achievement?"

"Is that a question or a statement?"

"I don't know. I thought it would make me feel like I made it. Like I accomplished something. It would be a sign that…I don't know, maybe…"

"That you were accepted?"

"Yeah, I guess."

"And the only thing that is missing from the list is a wife. If she is the final piece of the puzzle, what could she provide that all of this stuff couldn't?"

"Companionship?"

"Is that all? I think you had plenty of companionship? What else?"

I knew that I was missing something that was blatantly obvious to Dale. It's not as if she wasn't buying what I was giving her, but I could sense there was something I was totally missing. I started to recap my answer.

"Well, I would feel like I achieved something and that would make me happy," I said.

"I would..."

Dale sighed a bit, as if she were done playing around.

"Ryan, what did you want on the inside?" she asked. "All I'm hearing about are things on the outside. What did your heart want?"

"Ryan, what did you want on the inside?" she asked. "All I'm hearing about are things on the outside. What did your heart want?"

Now it was obvious. I guess I had thought that all of this accumulation and achievement would magically result in love.

Dale continued.

"And I'm not saying that some of the women in your past didn't love you. I'm sure they did. But how could they give you anything else than love for what Ryan had on the outside when that's all you gave them?"

It all made sense. It even sounded familiar. Yet I needed a moment to take it in.

"You only gave them a portion of you to love, the exterior. And since that is all they had to love, that's all they did love."

As I looked back on the women I had relationships with, I knew that statement was true.

Dale took it one step further. It was a critical step, something Dale had been driving at in previous sessions.

"It also sounds to me like what you ultimately wanted from these women was the exact thing you wanted from your Mom."

I just nodded my head.

"And you deserved that but let me ask you this: Do you think she loved herself on the inside?"

"No, I really don't."

"Then how could she give you something she didn't already possess? How can anyone give away something they don't already have for themselves?"

Cleveland

September 15 was a cold, rainy afternoon in Kansas City. The Royals were hosting the eventual world champion Chicago White Sox, wrapping up a short homestand. The season was less than three weeks from completion. No matter the year or my current state of mind, the end of the season is a relief. Once you reach the month of September, you start the countdown: Only 30 games left, three road trips left, I only have to pack my suitcase three more times, 15 more nights in a hotel and so on...

This year, in particular, I was counting the minutes. Not only was I looking forward to being home for some rest, I was also hoping the off-season would help in my recovery. The end of the season would mark one month of being on the medication. I could enter the off-season feeling like myself again. I had plans with friends. I had a couple of weddings to attend in Minnesota and Florida. Most of all, I wouldn't have to spend any more frighteningly lonely days in a hotel room.

After that cold game on September 15, the traveling party boarded the bus for the airport. We had a short trip to Cleveland for Friday, Saturday, and Sunday games, and would come right back home. I remember having a sense of fear about being on the road again but kept telling myself we'd be back in three days.

We landed, boarded buses, and headed for the hotel in downtown Cleveland. It was only about 8 PM when we arrived so I started to think about what I was going to do that night. In a different state of mind, I would have gone up to the room, settled in, watched some TV, and made a few phone calls. Now things were different. I was trying to minimize my time alone in the room. I picked up my room key and decided I would drop off my sport coat and briefcase, grab my cell phone, and walk around Cleveland all night.

I called Eric. He asked me how I was feeling and I told him the truth. I thought I was getting better, but I still had some bad days. He reminded me that I had been taking Lexapro for two weeks and that the meds take a month for full effect. When I told him that I was still relying heavily on Xanex, he became concerned and cautioned me about how addictive the drug can be. I tried as best as I could to sound upbeat, but I could tell he wasn't going for it. Again, I was disappointed by his opinion, but I appreciated his candor. He wasn't concerned about the Lexapro eventually working, but he was concerned about my reliance on the Xanex. It hadn't evolved into a dependency, but he made it very clear that I could be heading in that direction. After about an hour on the phone, we hung up and I called my Mom. Like Eric, she asked how I was doing. I told her I just wanted to get through these three days and get home. She said she would have her phone with her at all times if I needed her. After hanging up I felt I had enough courage to return to my room and get to bed. I didn't have much trouble falling asleep.

At this point, I was waking up around 2 AM on a fairly regular basis. Half of the time I was able to get back to sleep about 30 to 60 minutes after taking a Xanex. Other times I wasn't so fortunate. My short road trip got off to a roaring start when I woke up at 2 AM with that familiar pounding heartbeat, sweat-filled sheets, and racing mind. This had become a part of my normal routine so I wasn't immediately alarmed. But soon I felt that warm, tingling sensation build inside the center of my chest, the familiar announcement that a panic attack was on its way. My mind was at it again.

By now, placing the bottle of Xanex and a glass of water on the bedside table before I went to sleep was a part of my normal evening routine – open bottle, pop pill, drink water, lie back down, and let my mind beat me up until I was able to fall asleep again. Not so on this night. Panic spawned more panic. I couldn't even make it through the first night on the road. I still had two more nights

Eric was right. There was reason to be concerned, relying so much on Xanex. This added more panic. Before this night I looked forward to feeling normal again. On September 16 at 2 AM I started to truly doubt whether this was ever going to happen. I had forgotten what normal felt like. I couldn't even describe what the word calm meant. I had gone from fearing an institutionalized life to wondering if that might be the best option for me. Maybe I could get fixed before the 2006 season. If not, who cares? If putting me on a bed with white sheets, white walls, and being hooked up to an IV would make this pain go away, I would have taken it. By 5 AM my brain was like oatmeal. I had allowed these illusions to create a sense of reality. I was sure my life was over. I needed to find a way to get out of the next night's game. I decided that after everyone left the hotel around 4 PM for Jacobs Field, I would check myself into a local hospital. I wasn't sure what I would tell the nurse when I checked in but I figured they had two options: do something for me now or they could scrape me off the street later. One thing was for certain, I didn't want to die in a Marriott. Maybe I could spend a couple of nights in a hospital, my Mom would come in from New Mexico, and we could discuss whether I would spend the next couple of months in a hospital in Kansas City or Albuquerque. There was no way my little 10mg pills of Lexapro were going to fix this mess of a human spirit, no matter how long I was on the medication. I was done. It was over.

I was in and out of a light sleep for about five more hours. The curtains were closed tightly and by 10 AM my room was still as dark as a cave. I got out of bed a couple of times to use the bathroom but crawled right back into bed. I had gone without a good night's sleep for over a month. I was absolutely exhausted. The anxiety had affected my appetite and workout schedule. I was already at a point in the season when I was tired just because I had been going at it almost every day since March 1. Throw in the bonus material of an emotional breakdown and you can imagine how spent I was.

I knew I would have to wait at least six more hours before I could sneak through the lobby, undetected by the team, and head for the hospital. I called my Mom and told her I wasn't doing very well. I didn't share with her the check-myself-into-a-hospital plan because I didn't want to alarm her. I figured I could have a nurse from the hospital call her after I was admitted and explain that I was in good hands and couldn't do any harm to myself. That was my plan. I did share with Mom that I was starting to doubt whether I would get back to normal again. She understood and shared a few nearly identical feelings she experienced when she was in trouble. She convinced me that I should open the curtains in my room, get dressed and go for a long walk. I remember thinking to myself, "How did she know the curtains were closed?" What I needed, she explained, was some exercise and some fresh air. Opening the curtains would give the room a different look when I returned and would prevent me from wanting to crawl back into bed. I told her I would think about it.

"Just put one foot in front of the other and take baby steps."

She made me promise her I would take a walk and wouldn't hang up until I obliged. I agreed and told her I would call her after my walk. I hung up and got right back under the covers.

Now it was 10:30 AM. I still had five-and-a-half hours. I tried to go back to sleep but struggled to close my eyes and relax. Then it was 11 AM...five hours to go. I didn't want to make the call to get out of the game too soon because someone might come and check on me and notice I wasn't really sick. If they asked enough questions I knew I would fall apart. I just wanted to get to the hospital and get hooked up to an IV (at least that's what I envisioned). I'd rather be loopy from the medication in the hospital than bawling in front of someone from our medical staff in my hotel room. I had to wait until the training staff and broadcast team were gone and then I'd make the call.

At 11:30 AM I started to get hungry. I would have to eat eventually so I decided to take a walk for something to bring back to the room. I got dressed. Like Mom prescribed, I opened the curtains. Then I just sat on the foot of the bed. Sweat started to build on my forehead. The tingle and pounding heartbeat returned. I was afraid to leave my room. What had become a place where the demons of depression had their way with me became somewhat of a safe haven. Now I feared leaving my room. I just sat on the bed, bent over with my face in my hands.

What was happening to me? How did I get here?

Tears and intense sobbing followed. I thought about

the life I imagined: a wife and kids at Lake Winnebago. There would be big family Thanksgiving and Christmas dinners to look forward to. I was going to broadcast for the Royals for at least 25 more years.

Instead, I had become the percentile you rarely hear about that doesn't benefit from therapy and medication. There would be studies conducted on me. Doctors would use me as an example. Instead of going down as a great baseball announcer, my name would be linked to the seemingly healthy, happy, young adult who lost his mind.

Eventually the crying stopped. Now it was noon and I was still sitting on the foot of the bed. As it had so many times in the past month, the uncontrollable weeping provided some relief. I was still deeply depressed, but the fear had faded some. I wiped my eyes, cheeks, and forehead and stood up. I looked in the mirror above the bathroom sink to see if I appeared to be as insane as I felt. Aside from red eyes I didn't look too scary. I could still pose as a very pleasant person, at least for a short encounter. Any extended interaction would reveal the lonely soul inside. I pulled a hat over my head and opened my door. I looked out into the hallway to make sure nobody familiar was visible. Typically the Royals put all of the members of the broadcast team on the same floor. It's affectionately known as the Media Turd

Floor or MTF. It was safe to go to the elevator. I was trying to avoid communication with anyone. My emotions were still very close to the surface, and I was sure just about anything would set me off. Not only that but I was dealing with the whole new set of circumstances of trying to get past a fear of leaving my hotel room. The Marriott Key Center in Cleveland was undergoing a major remodeling, and the corridor of my floor had been redecorated with bright red and yellow carpet. With my senses intensified, I was startled by the colors as I opened my door. My heart pounded harder. After taking a deep breath, I left my room.

I got into the elevator, went down to the lobby, and exited the hotel through a side door. Nobody saw me. There was no face-to-face communication. Now I could concentrate on walking the streets of Cleveland.

Cleveland is nothing like New York City, but I felt the same sensations I had experienced just three weeks ago in midtown Manhattan. Everything seemed much louder and more crowded than I remembered. Mom was right, however; just getting some exercise helped. My anxiety lessened quite a bit as I continued to walk and take deep breaths of fresh, northern Ohio air. I picked up some food from a local sushi restaurant and headed back to the hotel. It was about 1 PM. I ate my delicious spread of raw fish in my hotel room. Lunch gave me an additional lift as it did in New York and Detroit. I called my Mom to tell her I had followed her instructions and that I was going to try to get ready for the game. Again no mention of the strategy I had planned earlier that morning. She seemed relieved but wanted me to check in with her before the game started. I agreed.

I abandoned the hospital plan, feeling as if I might have enough strength to make it through the game. As I boarded the bus for Jacobs Field, I was still fearful of whether I would make it but I also felt partly victorious that I had beaten my condition, albeit barely, for another day.

I always enjoy it when the Royals play the Indians because Cleveland's broadcast team is a bunch of great guys led by the longtime voice of the Indians, Tom Hamilton. Hammy is a great announcer and an even better person. When he asks, "How are you doing?" he means it. To say the least, I always look forward to seeing Hammy and the rest of the crew. Not on this day. I was sure a conversation with him would produce a crack in my already weak protective shell. As fate would have it, though, we crossed paths right before the game started.

"Boy, you've changed," I heard as I entered the stadium's media dining room.

It was Hammy.

"I remember when you used to come over and say hello," he said. "Now look at you."

"Hey Hammy, good to see you. Sorry, I've been rushed all day," I answered as I passed his table on the way to the food line.

"You been working out? How do you stay so skinny?"

"Clean living, Hammy, clean living"

Hammy let out one of his trademark roaring laughs.

I mention this short dialogue because it seemed from that day forward more and more people noticed I was losing weight. I wasn't skipping meals, and my workout schedule actually had become less intense, but I was losing weight.

I called Mom right before we went on the air, and I eventually got through the broadcast fine. The next morning I went to the hotel gym to step on the scale. I had lost 15 pounds in the past month. This gave me something else to think about as checking the scale became another one of my obsessions.

My condition improved the following day as it had after the rougher nights and days the past month. I was still in a deep depression but a lot of the anxiety had subsided. I got through the next two games and returned to Kansas City.

Fun?
What's Fun?

My bout with depression had triggered another condition called anhedonia (an'hē-dø'nē-ă). While having lunch with Eric in Chicago, I told him that my recovery seemed to be slowed by not being able to motivate myself to do the things I once enjoyed. This made my battle even more difficult because I couldn't counter my loneliness with anything but chores, exercise, and work. Eric explained that this was a common experience for those afflicted by depression. He had experienced the same, as had my Mom. Now I had a word I could attach to this sudden void in my life, anhedonia. Hedonism, as you probably know, is defined as living for the day, seeking personal pleasure as a priority. Anhedonia is virtually the opposite – the inability to experience pleasure.

People with anhedonia no longer recognize what was once pleasurable to them, so they don't seek out that pleasure. I was in the "inability to recognize" category. Once I was put into a pleasurable environment (usually because someone else initiated the outing) I quickly remembered the satisfaction. While alone, however, the desire to seek fun simply wasn't there.

People with anhedonia no longer recognize what was once pleasurable to them, so they don't seek out that pleasure.

Toronto

I love my job. I am so blessed to be in the small percentage of people in the world who are doing exactly what they want to do for a living. If I couldn't broadcast baseball for the Royals, I'm sure I would find something else to do eventually. But it would take some time for me to figure out what that "something else" would be. I don't have a list of things I'd rather be doing. I'm doing it.

With all of that being said, the Major League Baseball season is a grind. I know most people don't see it that way. But over the course of seven months, there are close to 180 broadcasts (including spring training), there are no weekends off, there is only one stretch of back-to-back days off (three or four days for the All Star break), there is working mostly nights and opposite everyone else's schedule, and there are four of those months living on the road. So as much as I love it, I'm ready for it to be over each September. I'm ready to be home for a long stretch without having to pack a suitcase or listen to my own voice calling a game.

In 2005 the season concluded with a three-game weekend series in Toronto. Prior to this series we spent four days in Minnesota, where I had no significant episodes of panic or depression. Having spent 10 years in Minnesota, I have several friends there and made sure my calendar was full of breakfast and lunch dates. After the problems I encountered in New York, Detroit, and Cleveland, I did what I could to avoid long periods of time alone in my hotel room. I was successful and felt cautiously optimistic when we boarded the plane in Minneapolis on our way to Toronto on September 29. I had a few moments of slight melancholy in Minneapolis, but I was four days away from the off-season and two days away from the one-month mark of taking Lexapro. I felt I was getting better.

As on the trips to New York and Detroit, we arrived in Toronto very late. I wasn't in bed until 4 AM. I wasn't too concerned because in a few days I could sleep in and take long naps in the afternoon. I slept very well that night/early morning. But when I woke up, I wasn't

Broadcasting the Royals' games took my mind off my worries for a few hours.

alone. The aching inside was right there.

I'm not sure if it was denial or just sheer determination to fight off this renewed sense of darkness, but I decided rather quickly that this wasn't depression. I was physically tired from the late arrival and figuratively tired of sitting in a hotel room feeling despair. Ten minutes after waking up I was dressed in workout clothes and out the door for a run along Lake Ontario. I figured all I needed was to get my blood and endorphins flowing and I would feel much better. I refused to listen to the lies. Without saying anything or using my hands, I was doing the equivalent of someone covering their ears and yelling, "La la la la la la" while someone else is trying to tell them something they don't want to hear. I got off the elevator and, just like Forrest Gump, "I just started running."

I was going to literally run this bad feeling into submission. I was going to sweat the lies out of my body. I ran hard and I ran for a long time, admonishing my demons with every stride. "Not today! You're messing with the wrong dude. You have no control over me. I know who I am and it's not what you say. You might as well find someone else." It was working.

Again, it was a display of how powerful the mind can be. After running myself and the lies into the ground, I returned to the hotel and ordered room service. I was going to eat lunch and prepare for the game at the same time. I turned on the television for some white noise and called my Mom, all in an attempt to avoid quiet time alone. After chatting with my Mom, my food arrived and I was eating and preparing for the Blue Jays. When that was completed I called Julee. I took a short nap. When I got up from the nap, I felt unusually calm and refreshed. "See, mind over matter," I said to myself. I jumped in the shower, got dressed, and headed for Rogers Centre.

That Friday night, September 30, I was in the television booth working with Royals Hall of Fame pitcher Paul Splittorff. I enjoy everyone I work with, and Paul is no exception. The Royals lost the game 10-1, but it was a quick whipping and we were back to the hotel at a decent hour. As a famous, former Royals manager once summed up, "If you're going to play horseshit, play fast."

The Royals played fast.

As I entered the room, I turned the TV on, answered a few phone calls and got into bed. I felt good. I felt that I had defeated depression that day. I was getting better. The season was almost over. The next day was going to mark one month on Lexapro. The worst was behind me.

The adrenaline didn't allow me to fall asleep as quickly as I would have liked. That meant I stayed awake in bed for almost an hour. The dreaded quiet time alone with my thoughts was back. The late morning run, positive conversations with Mom and Julee, and interesting broadcast with Paul had all run their courses and now the momentum was rapidly fading. I was trying hard to fall asleep to avoid the storm I could feel building inside. I could feel the familiar tingle.

All of a sudden the off-season started taking on a different light. What was intended to be a time of rest and recovery was now becoming a five-month sentence of solitary confinement at Lake Winnebago. I began to fear what was now just three days away. I could feel sweat building along my forehead. This wasn't supposed to be happening. I was feeling great just that morning. The tingling became that warm sensation in my chest, spreading to my neck, shoulders, and stomach. I tossed and turned in bed, desperately trying to find a comfortable position that would trigger sleep.

I started taking deep breaths and repeating to myself, "It doesn't mean anything. It doesn't mean anything." In a desperate attempt to escape another panic attack, I jumped out of bed to find my bottle of Xanex. After Minnesota, I had decided the bottle of Xanex and a glass of water on the bedside table was no longer a necessity. I turned the desk light on and rapidly searched my briefcase to find my only weapon the past two months, a prescription drug. I was going to pop two Xanex this time. That's right. I was going to kick this panic attack right in the groin. I rushed to the bathroom for a glass of water and...gulp. There was an immediate sense of relief. There was no way the drug had taken effect in three seconds but, again, it was the power of the mind.

I didn't want to take two Xanex one night before reaching the one-month mark of medication, but I had control of the situation and the panic attack couldn't take that away from me. Sure I might become dependent on this anti-anxiety medication, but for the moment, that was OK. I was in control. The anxiety and panic and depression had been controlling me for too long. Now it was going to be on my terms. I couldn't see my enemy, but I knew it was in the room. I got back into bed with my game face on. I closed my eyes and fell asleep almost immediately. It was about midnight. There was a lot of night left.

I learned more than I wanted about drug addiction and suicide about four hours later. No different from the experiences in New York and Cleveland, my condition woke me up in the middle of the night in a worse state of mind. What was different was that the double dose of Xanex gave me four hours of sleep rather than the normal two. Instead of revisiting my fears at 2 AM, I was awake at 4 AM. I was groggy from the drugs, yet wide awake when I looked at the clock.

Another major difference from previous middle-of-the-night encounters was how I felt. Instead of intense panic, with the sweat, pounding heartbeat, and clenching of my teeth and hands, this time I felt a sense of calm. Kind of like a politician who fights through a campaign, stays up all night waiting for the results to come in, experiencing the ups and downs of each polling station, but then realizes he or she has lost. They did all they could but didn't have enough votes in the end. It was 4 AM EDT on Saturday, October 1.

I had reached the one-month mark of medication and I wasn't cured. I fought through a tough campaign with depression, staying up all night at times waiting for some positive results. There were ups and downs. Yet as I stared at the ceiling, I rationalized that a lot of the ups were somewhat fabricated. I was mostly down. Now with the votes tallied after my month on medication, I was resigned to the fact that I had lost. There was very little panic. The so-called lies ended up being truth. I believe the sense of calm was an acceptance of where and what I was…defeated.

My drug and alcohol use in the past were partly recreational use and partly an escape from my insecurities. I had chosen to use these substances to change my state of mind. When I came to the conclusion that it was doing me and others more harm than good, it was easy for me to quit. This was much different. I believed that in order to continue my life I needed to be on some sort of mind-altering, anxiety-controlling drug. It no longer had to do with choice. I couldn't live like this anymore. I was convinced I was among the percentile of the severely depressed who didn't recover. Despite what my Mom, Eric, and my friend had promised, I couldn't be saved. I was beginning to understand why some people never quit addictions.

I've seen the documentaries. You know, perfectly normal people with perfectly normal upbringings living the life of a junkie? I used to ask all of the obvious questions. Why don't they quit? Don't they realize what they are doing to themselves? Why don't they get some help?

For several hours in my hotel room in Toronto on the morning of October 1, I knew why these people chose to live that way. They can't quit because they can't bear living with the hell inside their minds. Sure they realize what they are doing to themselves, but there is no other alternative. They don't try to get help because they are convinced it won't work. I empathized because the little hope I hung onto the past two months was dying in that hotel room in Toronto. Just to prove my point, I popped another Xanex.

It's so easy to say after the fact that suicide shouldn't be an option. I'm sure I've said it myself. We've all had moments when we "just felt like dying" and couldn't imagine facing the world again. We've all had moments of deep self-pity when we've said, "I'd be better off dead."

Suicide is usually followed by loved ones asking why the afflicted didn't tell anyone. It's normal to view the afflicted as being too weak to go on with life. "Perhaps if he was a little stronger, he'd be still with us," people say. Loved ones tend to blame themselves for not seeing the signs that led to someone ending their own life. When alcohol and drugs are involved, an impulsive decision can lead to suicide. In some cases the afflicted will commit suicide to make someone else hurt. Whatever the case, the afflicted doesn't view suicide as one option; it is viewed as the only option. On October 1, I found myself deciding rather calmly whether I wanted to go through the rest of my life dependent on drugs or in an institution to escape my madness, or just go be with God. One thing was for sure, I couldn't go on like this. In most discussions regarding severe depression, the most common way to describe the feeling is that it is indescribable.

I've never seen someone commit suicide, but I don't imagine it being like Mel Gibson's near suicide in the movie Lethal Weapon. Here Gibson is drinking and crying heavily over a picture of his late wife. It is very dramatic, but he doesn't go through with it. Instead, I imagine suicide being a decision one arrives at with great certainty. Again, it's not their first choice; it's their only choice.

I was remarkably calm as I continued to stare at the ceiling. The indescribable part of this horrid disease also makes it impossible to discover what ails you. If I had been afraid of losing my job, there would have been a reason and possibly a solution. If I had been afraid that the world was going to find out I had committed a crime, there would have been a reason and possibly a solution. If I had been afraid of losing a girlfriend, the same would have been true. There was that objective side of me that knew nothing was so horribly wrong in my life and that I should feel this way. It should be fixable. Then there was the more powerful subjective side that was convincing me that I was beyond repair. When the pain is unbearable and there is no hope, what's the sense of hanging around?

I never got so far as planning my own suicide, but I did consider the alternative of suicide. I simply did not want to live like this anymore. Suicide would be a drastic, last-ditch alternative for sure, but at least it was an option to end the pain. As insane as it may sound, the thought of having this option gave me some peace.

During my darkest days I thought often about a baseball teammate in high school, Sean Fitzpatrick. Fitz took his life while he was in college. I remember being told that he explained to his loved ones that he couldn't take the pain any more and wanted to be with God. That day in Toronto I knew how Fitz must have felt. I contemplated Fitz's words and fateful decision quite a bit on October 1. I thought about being with God in paradise and a long way from my agony.

Suddenly, though, I started to think about a couple of words I had been using often the past two months – God and hope. I was hoping I would recover from this pain and I was constantly talking to God. I was hoping God would hear my prayer and save me from this dark valley. Then I had another thought: If I get through this with God's grace, I can use this experience to give others hope. Wow. I don't know why that had never occurred to me before. I honestly had never looked at it that way: If I get through this, someone else might get through it, too.

I realized right at that moment that I might have a much bigger role to fulfill in this lifetime. That thought suddenly overcame me and the pain started to ease slightly.

I Am Alive!

I slept until about 10 AM and, as on the day before, I decided to get some exercise to fight off any anxiety. It wasn't easy but I had some conviction. I worked out at the hotel gym, and before I left I stepped on the scale inside the men's locker room. I was still 15 pounds underweight. Most people would be delighted with such a discovery, but I wasn't overweight back in early August. With this new information I had a high carbohydrate lunch, and was off to Rogers Centre for the late afternoon game with the Blue Jays. Denny Matthews, Fred White, and I shared the radio broadcast and enjoyed a thrilling Royals victory; it would be their last victory of the season. I felt pretty good the rest of the day and night. I had dinner with Fred and told him I had been experiencing the typical ups and downs, but that I was doing better. Once again he offered his and the Royals' support. On one hand I wasn't telling the truth, but on the other hand I had a new reason to be optimistic. I was going to defeat this, and use the experience to help others. It suddenly felt like I had a purpose again. This notion seemed like it was whipping my depression into some sort of submission. It was weird. And wild.

But it was short-lived. The demons of my depression were back that night. I opened my eyes at 5 AM on October 2, the last day of the 2005 season. You know the drill by now.

It was too early to call Mom or Julee for a pep talk. I reluctantly got out of bed and took a Xanex. I stayed in bed until 7 AM or so before doing my last round of pre-game preparation for the 2005 season. I packed my suitcase for the last time, showered and dressed, and checked out of our Toronto hotel. Any other year I would have had a noticeable bounce to my step as I completed all of these tasks for the final time of the season. It would have been all about sleeping in my own bed and not having to worry about suitcases or baseball for five months. Instead it was like a slow death march to my lonely and painful life in Missouri. What happened to my new sense of purpose? It was gone, in a flash.

My final broadcast of 2005 would be on television with Paul. On a TV day I would go straight to the production truck to discuss the show with our crew. On this Sunday, I arrived at Rogers Centre before they did. I was very anxious, and the symptoms of a panic attack were present. I spent some time in the seats near the Royals dugout as a high school All Star game was being played. Life seemed less complicated in high school. I thought life in high school was difficult at the time, but how I wished I could go back. I thought about how I would have done it again as I watched these young athletes compete on the field and pal around in the dugout. I thought about how driven I was in high school and college, and how that eventually drove me into the ground. I thought about all of the relationships I had let get away because they didn't jibe with what I wanted and where I was going. I also thought about all of the relationships I invested time and money in because I thought they would help get me where I wanted to go and what I wanted in life. I just shook my head and thought to myself, "Yeah, look at you now."

My phone buzzed in my pocket. It was Mom. She assumed that I was feeling the same as the day before and possibly even better since today was the last day of the season. I explained my setback, and she reassured me that I just needed to get through the game, get home, and get some sleep. She knew I hadn't had a good stretch of healthy sleep in about two months. I'm sure the sleep deprivation added to my condition, but simply having more time didn't automatically mean I would be able to relax. Fighting anxiety and depression for this long had left me with the conflicting feelings of exhaustion from the depression and energy from the anxiety. I wanted to sleep but my anxious mind wouldn't allow me. I wanted to remain active but the depressed soul wouldn't allow me. Many days I felt trapped with nowhere to turn.

After hanging up with Mom I decided to take a walk around the stadium to try to burn some of the anxiety off. I just had to get through one more game. It was a gorgeous day in Toronto and the air off Lake Ontario was very crisp and refreshing. I walked around the lower concourse twice asking God to give me the strength to get through this day.

I stopped by the production truck briefly to find out what our pre-game elements would be and headed to the broadcast booth. The panic was building and I did the best I could to avoid everyone. I found a table by myself in the dining room and ate quickly; before anyone had the chance to sit and join me. I walked down to the field as I normally would do before the game to gather some anecdotes and other tidbits for the broadcast. But on this day, I didn't gather any information. I was just trying to avoid sitting in one place, which might allow my anxiety to gather enough steam to trigger a breakdown.

One of the worst tricks depression plays on the mind – the demons convince you that the world is one great big, happy party. And you aren't invited.

About 45 minutes before game time I headed back to the booth. Paul hadn't arrived yet to tape our opening segment previewing the game. There is a door at the back end of the TV booth that leads to a private concourse for the stadium's luxury suites. This carpeted concourse is decorated with photographs of Toronto Blue Jays' historical moments and personalities, and it stretches half the diameter of the stadium. For the next 15 minutes I just walked back and forth alone in the concourse trying to focus on the photographs to take my mind off what was really going on. Of course all of the photographs were of celebrations and smiling faces, which just reminded me of how miserable I was. One of the worst tricks depression plays on the mind – the demons convince you that the world is one great big, happy party. And you aren't invited.

I returned to the TV booth, taped the segment with

Paul, and broadcast the final game of the 2005 season without incident. The exhaustion got the best of me, and I slept for the entire bus ride to the airport and most of the flight back to Kansas City.

The Truman Sports Complex in Kansas City is the enormous site that is home to both Kauffman Stadium (Royals) and Arrowhead Stadium (Kansas City Chiefs). We arrived at the complex shortly after the Chiefs completed a game with Philadelphia. I had plans for later that evening with a woman I had been seeing for a few months. The relationship had been running on fumes and was not intimate enough for me to share my situation, at least in any depth. She had attended the Chiefs game that day and we had plans to get together once I got back from Toronto. The bus pulled up to Kauffman Stadium with no sign of her. I walked to my truck and drove back to the front of the stadium to pick up my suitcase for the last time. When I emerged from the stadium and walked to my truck, there was still no sign of her. I climbed into my truck and absolutely snapped. This wasn't the type of snap I so frequently experienced the past two months. There was no panic. There were no tears. I was pissed off.

I called Julee and vented to her for about 20 of the 35 minutes it took me to drive home. Julee did the listening and I did the yelling. All of the frustrations of the past two months flowed out of me like water blasting out of a fire hose. Anger had arrived, ambushing and overwhelming the demons of my anxiety and depression. My blood was pumping and it was boiling. I was raging. I hadn't felt that good in a long, long time. I was alive!

For the first time in almost two months, that pit in the stomach that comes with the emptiness of depression was gone. The constant heaviness of being controlled by my thoughts was lifted away. The slouching posture of a young man who had lost hope was straightened out. At 7 PM on October 2, I was back. As incredible as it sounds, that fit of anger jerked me into a new reality. It's possible the anger triggered some chemical response that actually helped me. Who knows? But I swear, at that moment, after I had let out all that anger, I felt wonderful. Like a changed man.

By no means am I suggesting anger as therapy to combat anxiety and depression. But something happened to me that day.

If depression can be described as anger turned inward, then my recovery was greatly assisted that night because my anger was finally turned outward.

Prior to that night I was too depressed and too weak to do anything but hold onto my anger. The strain of doing so for two months slowed my healing.

Now this anger was like a spiritual purging of all the emotional toxins that had been eating up my mind and my soul. There was a strong sense of emotional and spiritual freedom.

My recovery was far from complete. But this was the most significant step to date.

I never experienced another panic attack after that night. Not one. By not meeting me as planned that night at the stadium, that former girlfriend may have saved my life.

Admitting the Problem

It may not be for everyone, but church has always been a place of hope for me. As I approached the front doors of Holy Spirit Catholic Church on Sunday, October 9, I saw the familiar faces in my church community. Most congratulated me for completing another 100-loss baseball season. "I'll bet you're glad it's over," my friend, Thomas Jewitt, said as he extended his right hand. I grabbed his hand and said, "Freedom. No more suitcases. No more airplanes."

After I entered the church our deacon, Rich Akins, came over to give me a congratulatory handshake, "Well, you got through it."

"Yes," I said, trying to smile, "I'm a free man."

For the next five months I would be free from the

rigors of the relentless baseball season. I was getting better, much better, but I knew I wasn't out of the emotional prison completely. The anger from the week before helped, but I certainly didn't feel completely free.

The off-season allowed me to attend Sunday morning Mass on a regular basis again. I needed some hope because I knew there was a lot of free time ahead of me, and I was still uneasy about being alone.

I'm Catholic. I believe there are many religions or places of worship that promote a productive, empathetic, and compassionate lifestyle. I just find peace in the rituals of the Catholic Mass.

Father Michael Tierney approached the altar as the congregation sang the opening hymn. Fr. Tierney is a wonderful communicator. We've become friends over the years, but I still appreciate him the most when he preaches. I really needed something from him that inspired me on this October Sunday.

Before Mass got going, the congregation was seated, and Fr. Tierney announced that he would perform the ritual of anointing the sick of the parish. "If anyone wants to be anointed, I ask that you stand. I also ask that those of you standing nearby to place your hands on the sick member of the church as a symbol of your blessing and support."

I've never really looked up the actual definition of who qualifies to be anointed but I figured it was reserved for someone who was gravely ill. Never in my-34 and-a-half years had I ever even considered being anointed. That changed on October 9. I was feeling better but I knew how gravely ill my mind was.

Fr. Tierney made his way down the aisles. Just about everyone standing was elderly. The sight of a member of my church family being anointed made me stop and think like never before. I thought about the humility of the afflicted person to acknowledge the helplessness, the courage it took to stand in front of other church members as a way of announcing a grave illness, the confident and comforting look on Fr. Tierney's face as he said the prayer of the anointing and made the sign of the cross with the oil, the look of hope on the anointed person's face after receiving the sacrament, and the faces of the loving and concerned friends, family, and strangers standing and placing their hands on the afflicted person. I have to admit I felt a little overwhelmed.

I wanted to stand. I really did. I wanted to acknowledge the helplessness of my condition. I wanted to see that look on Fr. Tierney's face up close, his eyes meeting mine. But I didn't have the courage. Nobody at that church knew of my condition that morning. If I would have stood up, I thought I might have caused a scene.

I shouldn't have cared about that. This is my church family, whether I know everyone there or not. This is why we come together on Sundays, right? I have faith. Yet my ego was more powerful than my faith, and I remained seated. That's all I thought about the rest of the Mass and the rest of the day. I obviously was ashamed of my depression, and I was ashamed that I didn't have the strength and the humility to expose myself that day. For three days, I couldn't get that feeling of shame out of my head. Why couldn't I step forward and admit my problem to everyone? Why couldn't I put my stupid ego aside? The feeling of shame wouldn't go away.

Finally, three days later, I approached Fr. Tierney and told him about my experience. He anointed me.

TLC

I was relieved to be home with the season completed, and I was conservatively optimistic about some recent breakthroughs. But looming ahead had been the TLC gala on October 14.

Temporary Lodging for Children is a transitional shelter for homeless, abused, and neglected children in Kansas City. I had visited the children at TLC in the past to encourage them, but usually I left feeling inspired by their stories and their hope for a better future. The foundation had asked me a few months earlier if I would serve as a spokesman for their organizational video and then emcee their annual fundraising gala. I agreed, but this had been well before my breakdown.

I knew I was getting better. The first two weeks of the off-season went quite well. I forced myself to start painting again. I played a round of golf in a charity event. I went to lunch with friends. My therapy with Dale continued with encouraging results. I was researching some volunteer opportunities that would occupy my time and hopefully have an impact in the community. I was so afraid of my mind playing tricks on me while I was alone at home that I made sure I wasn't home alone very often. It was working. Nonetheless, when I was reminded of the TLC gala, I wasn't confident that I was ready for something like that. Looking back at the New York incident, I was fearful of being in a setting with a large group of people I didn't know. This could be even worse because now all eyes would be on me. What if I lost it on the podium? I was still having my down moments in between the end of the season and the gala. Those moments were becoming less prevalent but I still didn't want to set myself up for a backslide. I thought about coming up with a reason I couldn't attend the gala but, in the end, I decided against that for a few reasons.

First, there wasn't much time for TLC to find another emcee (they had already printed the programs with my name in them). Second, they had since asked me to tell the 900 guests about my visits to TLC in order to encourage others to volunteer their time. Third, I knew I would eventually have to face a large crowd and emcee an event. I explained my concerns to Mom and she reminded me once again about getting on with my life, one foot in front of the other, one day at a time.

For the last few days leading up to October 14, I felt more confident in my ability to survive the evening.

I arrived early on October 14 at the Overland Park, Kansas, Convention Center to go over the program with

the director of the event. I was very anxious. I had some Xanex ready to go if needed, but I was determined not to use them unless I started to see spiders crawling out of people's eyes. The reception area outside the banquet hall was filling up and it was loud. I was starting to feel some panic symptoms but they were manageable. A few people began to enter the hall, and a nice young woman asked me if I would talk to her husband, who was a huge Royals fan. I agreed and used this situation to keep my mind off being anxious about the event.

The banquet hall continued to fill up, and all of the noise in the reception area spilled in. My table was right in front of the stage. I met a few couples as they sat down at the table. It was time to announce the five-minute warning for everyone to be seated. When that was finished I just sat on the stairs near the audio man, Duc Pham, and struck up a conversation with him. This kept me away from the crowd and the noise and, I believed, a panic attack. Then it was time to announce the three-minute warning. Again, I chose to hang out with Duc. Then, the one-minute warning. Chatting with Duc kept me calm. Now it was time to begin the program.

Anyone who has emceed a banquet knows that the first couple of minutes are crucial for the host. You are expected to warm up the crowd with a few jokes and get everyone in a lighthearted frame of mind before you get into the meat and potatoes of the program. I introduced myself and received a nice round of applause. I wasn't expecting this reaction, so I couldn't poke fun at getting no response. I must say, though, the applause was just what I needed. If I never again receive applause at a banquet for introducing myself…fine. I needed it on that night. I told my first joke and got a great response. Joke number two also worked. Joke number three was the best, and I decided to move on from there. It felt like old times. No anxiety or panic whatsoever. After directing the folks to begin their meals, I explained we would resume the program in about thirty minutes. Again, another round of applause. Honestly, I didn't do anything special to begin the program that night. I felt comfortable and the audience had a good sense of humor.

I smiled at Duc as I returned to my table and met the rest of the group. They were a friendly bunch and complimented me on my opening and for my work as a Royals announcer. I needed that, too. We began to eat when I realized that everyone at my table was a married couple. I was sitting next to the only empty chair. My brief euphoria took a hit when I was reminded that I was alone.

After 30 minutes, I returned to the podium to tell a personal story about a visit I had at TLC that touched my heart. After that I was to acknowledge some special guests, direct the awards ceremony, and then introduce the keynote speaker, Linda Armstrong Kelly. Mrs. Kelly is the mother of bicycle champion Lance Armstrong. She had just released a book about her life as a single mother raising Lance.

I had some points I wanted to make during my personal story about a visit to TLC but I kept thinking about that empty chair. I couldn't remember what points I wanted to make but I told the story about a courageous 6-year-old girl who had been abandoned. I just spoke from my heart because it had become quite heavy. I'm an emotional person as it is, so for me to get a little choked up over sentimental stories is no new thing. I did have to stop a couple of times during my presentation to gather myself. As I paused with my head down, I could see that empty chair at my table. It was no different from any other chair among the patrons, but to me it stood out like it was lit with neon signs. I had everyone's attention, and I knew they were hanging on every word, hoping I could finish the story. Yet I felt alone. This particular audience caught me at a time of my life when I was totally transparent, unable to hide my feelings. That night I was emotionally exposed.

I got through the program and enjoyed introducing Linda. She told a wonderful story about her life and her devotion to her eventual seven-time Tour de France champion and cancer-surviving son. It was a wonderful night for TLC. But it wasn't over.

I was ready to get to my car and go home. I wasn't ashamed of displaying my emotions, but I still felt a little embarrassed. I was also mentally and emotionally drained from all of the worrying I had done leading up to the gala. But I couldn't get out of the banquet hall. I had people lined up to thank me for sharing my TLC story. Total strangers saying they wanted to shake my hand or give me a hug for delivering such a heartfelt message.

"TLC is blessed to have someone like you telling their story."

"The Royals should be proud to have you representing them in the community."

"Kansas City is fortunate to have you. I hope we don't lose you."

"That was a wonderful story. Thank you so much for sharing it with us."

Linda Armstrong Kelly also gave me a big hug and told me my mother should be proud of me. She then gave me a free signed copy of her book with a very thoughtful message.

All of this sounds self-promoting and I don't intend for it to sound that way. I mention these compliments not to inflate my own ego. I mention it because on one of the most important days for the TLC foundation and for me in the Kansas City community, I couldn't ward off my own feelings of loneliness. I became consumed with the thought that on this special night, I had nobody special to share it with. With every compliment I heard after the banquet, I became more distant. I was smiling and grateful on the outside but I felt more and more alone on the inside.

I finally got to my car and called my Mom to tell her I needed to come home. Two mornings later I was on a plane headed for New Mexico.

Therapy

Dale sat back in her chair and stared at me for a moment without saying anything. Then she asked, "So, let's take a look at how you see yourself?"

"Well, I think I have some things going for me," I said.

"OK, continue," she said, as she started writing on her yellow legal pad.

"I guess I'm decent looking," I said. "I have a good job. I like my job. I have a nice house..."

I looked up at Dale and I could tell she was a bit discouraged by my answers.

"Let me try asking this question again," she said. "How do you feel about yourself on the inside?"

"I feel alone. I feel empty. I feel like I'm going to be alone for the rest of my life because who would ever want to be around someone as messed up as I am. I'm a failure. I had a plan but it has produced nothing."

Dale was letting me vent. I was running at the mouth and she was writing down notes at a great pace.

"I feel like I don't fit in," I continued. "I feel unhealthy. I feel very selfish and inconsiderate..."

Suddenly, Dale stopped me and asked, "How so?"

"How do I feel selfish and inconsiderate? Well, my Mom has been with me every step of the way through this and then I have spent so much of my time with you blaming her."

"Are we blaming her? Do you blame her?"

"No, I really don't. I mean, I don't think I do. But when we keep going back in time, I keep having visions of things that she did or didn't do."

Dale put the pad down and took a deep breath.

"OK," she said, "Let me ask you a question. Do you blame your Mom? Is she the only reason why you are here?"

This began to anger me.

"No," I said, almost defensively.

"Why?"

"Because it wasn't all her fault."

"How so?"

"Well, as I go through all of this stuff in the past, I realize that she probably missed out on a lot of what she needed when she was a little girl. Her life is a lot like mine."

"Do you think, on the inside, your Mom felt any better when you were a child than you do now?"

"No, I don't. I think she felt just as horrible. But she had a son to raise. And she didn't always surround herself with people who cared about what was going on inside of her. And maybe she didn't have the resources that I have today to work on this stuff."

"Did you surround yourself with people that cared for the desires of your heart?"

"Not always, no."

"Do you think your Mom loved you?"

"Of course, I do."

"Do you think she cared about your well-being?"

"Yes, I do."

Dale had a somewhat satisfied look on her face. We were making some sort of progress yet I felt like I was still in full defense of my Mom.

"Do you think your grandmother loved your Mom?" Dale asked.

"Yes."

"Do you think she cared about your Mom's well-being?

"Yes."

"Then why do you suspect your Mom had some pain left over from her childhood?"

"Because, I don't know, I sensed that maybe my Mom wanted more but didn't receive it."

"Do you think your grandmother did the best she could raising your Mom?"

I heard the question but didn't answer it right away because I was slowly experiencing a moment of epiphany. I didn't say anything for about a minute.

"You know what, Dale," I finally said. "My grandmother is a good woman. I truly believe that. But more than anyone else, she is most impressed with my success. She is a classic name-dropper. For years, she carried around some of my college baseball cards and passed them out to her friends. I thought it was a little over the top at the time but I just kind of laughed it off. I figured she was just being a proud grandmother. Yet I can see it so clearly now. Her image was always very important to her and she probably expected the same things out of her loved ones.

Even though my grandmother loved her children, I think my Mom kind of inherited that sense of image from her mother. Certain material successes mattered to keep that image. My Mom and her brother have had stages of their lives where they were flashy and that was important to them. I don't think my Mom wanted to pass on that sense of image, and the pain that comes with it, but she did."

“Was that her goal?”

“No. I think that was all she knew.”

“Did she actually teach you this sense of image or did you just pick it up from her?”

“I picked it up from her.”

“With what she had, do you think your grandmother did the best she could, with whatever inside wounds she may have had, to love and raise your mother?”

“Yes, I think so.”

“And do you believe your Mom…”

For maybe the first time in our sessions, I interrupted Dale.

“I know where you’re going with this,” I said. “Yes, I do believe my Mom did the best that she could, with all of her unresolved pain, to raise me.”

“Remember when we talked about not being able to give what we don’t already possess?”

“I do.”

“Is it possible that your mother wasn’t able to give to you what you needed on the inside until she found it for herself?”

“Yes.”

“That’s why this can be confusing. Today, your Mom gives you everything you desire from a mother. She is there for you. You can rely on her. She takes care of you. But when you were a little boy, you felt disconnected and abandoned. So the little boy inside of you still carries around some pain and you are triggered by that little boy because he still needs his mother."

I was silent.

"Ryan, you have told me in the past that you think you've hurt some women. Did you love them? Did you care about their well-being?"

I just nodded.

"Did you do the best you could, with the pain you had?"

Another nod.

"This is not an excuse for hurtful behavior. For that matter, it's not an excuse for your grandmother's or your mother's behavior. You are all adults now and expected to make adult decisions. But can you give your mother some grace for some of her poor choices?"

"Yes."

"Can you give yourself some grace?"

"Yeah, I think I can."

"And I believe you should. Is it possible that your mother felt...," Dale said as she looked at her notes, "alone, empty, like she was going to be alone for the rest of her life because who would ever want to be around someone as messed up as she was? Do you think she felt like a failure, like she had a plan and it produced nothing?"

I didn't say anything but I understood. And I felt sadness, for my Mom.

"Do you think there were times when she didn't fit in? By the way, what did you do when you didn't feel like you fit in?"

"I used alcohol and drugs to fool myself into feeling that way."

"Did your mother do that?"

"I think she did."

"So, if we can assume that your Mom felt some of the same things about herself that you feel today, is she that person now?"

"No."

"Why?"

"Because she just isn't. That's just how she felt. And she did a lot of work to get herself past that. She's nothing like those words."

"So were those truths or lies running around her head?"

"Mostly lies."

"And what about you? Are those truths or lies?"

In Mother's Arms

Nobody else was at my house when I drove away at 5 AM on Sunday, October 16, but I felt as if I were leaving someone behind – perhaps it was the vision of what my life was supposed to be. I felt like I was sneaking away from something in the morning darkness. I needed to be with my family, especially with my Mom who had shared most of the pain of this nightmare with me. It's an hour drive from Lake Winnebago to Kansas City International Airport, and I had plenty of time to think about where I was going, literally and figuratively. I had that familiar empty feeling inside, but no sign of anxiety at all.

I arrived at the airport, boarded the plane and slept for almost the entire flight from KC to Albuquerque.

When I woke up prior to landing, I still felt somewhat uneasy with a mix of emotions. I knew I was getting better but I still didn't recognize if there would be any joy for the rest of my life. I wondered (and worried) if I was falling back into a deep depression. I just wanted someone to tell me I was going to be OK. I wanted someone to tell me it was all going to go away. I just needed someone, period.

The plane landed and all I wanted was my Mom. I needed my Mom. It seemed like forever for the plane to pull up to the gate. Like a bathtub slowly filling up with water, I could feel the tears were slowly building inside of me since the moment I left my house that morning. I got off the plane as quickly as I could. I had a hat on with the bill pulled as low as it would go to hide my face and eyes. As I left the gate I picked up my pace, trying to get to the terminal before the water reached the top edge of the tub and poured all over the place. I must have looked like one of those speed-walkers you pass in the morning on the way to work.

I was just about to reach the terminal when I spotted Mom. She was by herself, standing off to the right side. She could see the pain in her little boy's eyes. As I got closer I could see the love and concern all over her face. Lips together, she tried to smile but it was more of a look of concern. I couldn't get there fast enough. She tilted her head to the side and reached her arms out to me. I couldn't walk fast anymore. I ran the last four steps right into her arms. With my face buried into her right shoulder, the tears rolled onto her like a small waterfall. I couldn't remember the last time I had a shoulder to cry on, but I drenched her sweater for at least two minutes. Mom held me tight with her left arm and gently stroked the back of my head with her right hand. Then I felt something I hadn't experienced for a very long time. I felt safe. It was as if I was a little boy again and Mom was there to protect me. I don't remember if she said anything to me but it sure felt like: You're OK, Honey. Mommy's right here. Everything is going to be just fine. I'm right here.

I had never felt safer in my life than I did for those two minutes in the middle of the Albuquerque International Airport. Right there, in my mother's arms.

The break through

I spent four days in Albuquerque with my Mom, my step-father Jimmy, and my half-brother Travis. I was an emotional wreck. Jimmy and Travis were comforting and offered their support but I needed to be with Mom. Even though we had been fairly close ever since I left for college and extremely close the past 10 years, it felt like my Mom and me were making up for lost time. I felt like a cub wanting to stay close to its mother; keeping her within constant eyesight. I went to the local fitness center one day – Mom came with me. I wanted to run at the high school track another day – Mom brought a book. Every time she left the house to run an errand, I went with her. She sat with me in bed every night before I went to sleep, encouraging me and listening to whatever was on my mind. The tears flowed constantly, but I wasn't sure why. There was no anxiety or panic. I was armed with Xanex, just in case, but I never needed it. For the first time in my life I felt like I had my Mom and that was all I needed.

But I sensed all along that this trip to Albuquerque had a much bigger purpose, something that might alter my perspective for the rest of my life. The critical day was Tuesday, October 18. Though it wasn't really preplanned on my part, it turned out, in retrospect, to be the most important day of my recovery. Mom had suggested we take a hike at the base of Sandia Mountain. The weather was gorgeous. The scenery was breathtaking. And as the day progressed, I felt an urging inside to take a major step forward in my recovery. I was going to strengthen the bond between my Mom and I.

We hiked and talked quite a bit that day and when we decided it was time to head back to the car, we stopped to sit and relax. I had been sharing details of my therapy with Mom ever since I visited Dale's office for the first time. Mom knew that there were some issues related to her but she never pressed me about what they might be. She knew that I was dealing with a detachment from her that went all the way back to the age of 4. But she didn't know about the specific events that Dale took me back to.

I explained that my search for a loving and caring wife was actually a misguided search for the Mom that I wanted comfort and assurance from as a young child.

As we sat there in this beautiful setting, I began to share with Mom the moments of my childhood that scarred me. I explained that feeling distant from her led to the true beginnings of my fear of abandonment. I explained that my search for a loving and caring wife was actually a misguided search for the Mom that I wanted comfort and assurance from as a young child. I must have rambled on for almost 30 minutes. My Mom didn't say a word during this time.

When I finished, I looked up and I was somewhat surprised by my Mom's reaction: She nodded, almost knowingly. She said she had suspected this was part of the problem. And she said she had been waiting to actually hear the words come out of my mouth. She didn't cry but I could tell she was saddened to think she was connected to the root of the problem. But, having been through therapy herself, she also appeared to be relieved, knowing full well that the most important part of recovery is diagnosing the problem.

"Is that it?" she asked, while looking straight at me.

"No. There have been other things I've had to sort through, but these things have been the biggest issues."

"I don't know what to say."

"You don't have to say anything. That was a long time ago, and there's nothing either one of us can do about it now."

She knew I was right. It was Mom who constantly reminded me that we can't do anything about the past. All we can do is deal with the present.

"That's why we call the present a gift," she would say often.

"But Mom, I want you to know a couple of things. I never could have gotten through this without you. Whenever I needed you, you were there. I also want you to know that I forgive you. I know how hard life was for you then. I didn't understand it as a child but I understand it now. I understand now how much you were hurting inside. And I want you to know that if God came down from heaven and offered me any mother in the world, I'd tell Him I wanted you. I'm so proud to have you as my Mom."

Mom smiled, looked right into my eyes, and then put her arms around me.

"Thanks, Honey."

I could tell she believed me. Tears rolled down my cheeks. I told her I loved her. We decided to head back to the car.

I decided to leave the pain of my childhood at that spot on Sandia Mountain.

An Old Friend

I returned to Kansas City for a couple of days before leaving again, this time for a wedding in Minnesota.

I arrived in Minneapolis on Friday, October 21, to read scripture at my friend Dave Dover's wedding. As at the TLC gala, I was contemplating excuses for why I couldn't make it. As at the TLC gala, I knew it was too late to get out of this commitment, and I knew I needed to be there for Dave and for me. Minnesota was my home for 10 years and it still feels a little like home every time I visit.

After landing, I went to the Avis counter at Minneapolis/St. Paul International Airport and was informed that I qualified for a special weekend upgrade. For a few more bucks a day, the agent explained, I could go from a full-size car to a luxury car.

"Oh yeah? What do you got?"

"Well sir, you can have either a Lincoln Town Car or a Cadillac."

I figured I deserved a little luxury after all I had been going through.

"I'll take the Cadillac."

"You know that comes with satellite radio."

"Perfect."

So I was on my way to the wedding rehearsal in my battleship-sized Caddy with smooth jazz vibrating out of the premium sound speakers. Music with no words: That suited my mood. Life was pretty good at that moment. I pulled up to the church just as the rehearsal had begun.

My role was pretty simple. I just had to get up from my seat and read from the lectern a couple of times. I wasn't an actual member of the wedding party. Still, I was invited for the rehearsal.

I walked into the church, crossed myself with holy water, and introduced myself to the rest of the wedding party. The church was medium-lit and very serene. I saw Dave and his fiancée, Julie, standing in front of the altar talking to the wedding director. There was little noise except for a few distant voices and the soloist working out a few notes with the pianist. I took a seat in the back of the church not knowing I was going to be surprised by an old friend.

Dave and Julie held hands as they joked with the wedding director and pastor. I remembered Dave's broken engagement to another woman about six years earlier and how devastated he was. I remembered all of the failed attempts at relationships he had since and all of the times I tried to encourage him to keep his faith. I remembered the time I lectured him after he boldly told me he had given up on the thought of marriage. Now there he was, less than 24 hours away from marrying the love of his life.

I thought to myself how wonderful it was for him. But instead of being depressed about it, I felt as if there was hope for me, too.

Yes, an old friend – hope – surprised me with a visit that night in the back of St. Edward's Church in Bloomington, Minnesota. It had been so long I hardly recognized the feeling. There was no fear or anxiety. I felt complete peace. It was as if the past few months were a bad dream. I always preached hope to my friends during their times of despair. My recent illness, however, had expelled all of my hope. I didn't really realize it had been gone until it returned home that day. I realized I was going to be OK. I got through the emotional time in Albuquerque without any need for Xanex – this marked the 20th day of no Xanex. My therapy with Dale had revealed so much more than I ever could have hoped for. I had a better understanding and appreciation for who I was. I had a breakthrough experience with my mother. There was no anger, no resentment, no judgment in my heart. I realized I wasn't so interested in being in control or being right. I reflected upon how many friends had come to my rescue during this most difficult time of my entire life.

As these thoughts ran through my mind I kept my eyes fixed on Dave and Julie. Their union represented hope for me. I knew there was a reason I needed to be at that wedding.

Fleetwood

I was beginning to feel so much better about everything when one of life's sad and random moments hit me on October 29. I was driving home from Julee's annual Halloween party at her family's horse barn less than a mile from my house. Every year Julee and her husband, Jerry, invite neighbors, friends, and their children for a barbecue and bonfire. It was a brisk night, ideal to fill up the stomach at the grill and warm the bones at the bonfire. Aside from a few short conversations with neighbors, I spent the evening alone with my thoughts, which was fine. I knew I was getting better, much better, but I still needed some direction, and I spent most of the night thinking about upcoming plans.

On my way home around 10 PM, I spotted what appeared to be someone walking alone along the unlit streets around Lake Winnebago. As I looked to the right side of the road to see who it was, I noticed it was a woman. Though I recognized many of the people from the neighborhood, I didn't recognize her. She was holding a red retractable dog leash in her right hand. But there was no dog attached to the leash. As my eyes turned back to the road in front of me, I was stunned by a flash of gold fur bolting from the left side of the street and directly in front of my car. Before I could slam on the brakes, I ran right over a dog.

I didn't just hit the dog, I ran right over it. As I stopped the car, I came to grips with what had happened. I knew there was no way that the dog could have survived the impact. I jumped out of my car and looked around. The woman was already standing over her motionless golden retriever.

"Fleetwood! Fleetwood!" she cried.

I didn't know what to say, except, "I'm so sorry. I'm so, so sorry. I never saw him."

She crouched down and began to gently shake the dog.

"Fleetwood! Come on buddy, move for me!" she cried.

"Can I do anything?"

"Move for me Fleetwood!"

If this were a person, at least I could get on my cell phone and call 9-1-1.

"What can I do?"

"There's nothing we can do," she said, looking up at me. "I'm a nurse and I can feel his heartbeat. It's very slow and weak."

"I'm so sorry."

"It's all my fault. I didn't have him on a leash. I called him over to me."

The woman continued to caress Fleetwood.

"Oh, it's all my fault! I'm so sorry, Fleetwood!" she said, sobbing.

"Do you want me to call someone for you?"

"Oh Fleetwood, buddy," she said as she laid her head on top of his. Fleetwood looked just like my own golden retriever, Casey. He took his last breath and died, right in the middle of the street, under the flashing glow of my yellow hazard lights.

Later that night, after I'd arrived home, I sat very still on my bed. I felt awful for what had happened, and I felt a great sadness for my neighbor. This was such a different pain than the one I'd felt the past few months. This was the pain we all know from seeing someone else experience a loss. I thought about the woman quite often over the next few months. In a strange way, in a very selfish way I'm sure, it became part of my recovery process. For the first time in a long time, I got away from myself, away from my own issues, away from me. Someone else's grief overtook my own.

Sanibel

My first year with the Royals in 1999 was a very lonely year. I wasn't very popular my first year in Kansas City. The team lost 97 games and nobody wanted to listen to the new guy call the games. They wanted Fred White. Most people with the Royals and the radio network were supportive, but very few wanted to hitch their wagon to me in 1999. I can't blame them for that.

Nate Bukaty was one of my first Kansas City friends in 1999. By 2005, for a number of different reasons, Nate and I had drifted apart. We were still friends but didn't spend much time together away from work. We used to spend quite a bit of time at a jazz bar in Kansas City called "The Phoenix." At least once a week Nate and I, along with whoever was available, would go to The Phoenix to listen to live music and have deep discussions about politics, women, sports, relationships…you name it.

As I thought about my recovery, I spent quite a bit of time trying to rediscover all of the things that once made me a balanced person (at least in my eyes). I kept getting back to those nights at The Phoenix with Nate and friends. After returning home from my trips to New Mexico and Minnesota, I felt as if I needed to take some immediate action toward rediscovering those good times. I made a phone call to Nate explaining how much I appreciated him back in 1999 when I needed a friend and how I needed those days again. We made plans to revisit the place that helped build our friendship. What a great place to symbolize finding Ryan and putting him back together – The Phoenix. My favorite hangout in Kansas City was named after the mythological bird known for the ability to rise from its own ashes and fly again. Corny, yes, but I felt like I was flying again.

Being at The Phoenix brought back so many good memories. When Nate and I arrived there, the place was packed, the music was great, and everyone seemed to be having a good time. It wasn't until the drive home that I realized I hadn't felt crowded or anxious. I had no feelings even close to that. It felt like home again. I was starting to really feel like myself again.

I felt rejuvenated. I spent most of that week calling on friends and making plans to be social again.

The following weekend I attended the wedding of a good friend, Gordy Gutowsky. Gordy and I became friends through his father, John Gordon. John is a radio announcer for the Minnesota Twins and was my mentor. Gordy and I became close friends over the years and he, like Dave Dover, experienced some devastatingly painful breakups. But now I was going to be in his wedding on November 11 on Sanibel Island in Florida.

Sanibel Island is ideal that time of the year: 85 degrees, and, naturally, almost always sunny. We stayed in condos about 50 yards from the beach. The wedding was equally perfect. I wasn't going back to KC for another two days so I had all of November 12 to relax on Sanibel Island and enjoy the sand and sunshine. It ended up being one of the most productive days in years.

I had just started reading a book my step-dad, Jimmy, had given to me, Living with Joy, by Sanaya Roman. I read the third chapter that Saturday titled "You Can Live Joyfully." The chapter discussed something that had become a common theme in my recovery from anxiety-depression: Living in the present. A lot of my anxiety stemmed from focusing too much and worrying too much about the future. The chapter continued by challenging the reader to look at how he or she was using their time. Are we spending enough time doing the things that bring us joy? Do we even remember what brings us joy? Are we putting off our joy? This was a perfect chapter to sink into on the beach of Sanibel Island. At the end of the chapter, the author asks the reader to list things you love to do, things that bring joy to your life. Then list the reasons why you haven't been doing those things the last several months. For me it was more like the last several years.

It didn't take me long to fill the worksheet with several things I used to enjoy doing. My reason for not doing most of these things anymore was a lack of motivation. Either I didn't have the desire to organize one of these activities or I didn't think my friends were interested anymore. The book then suggested I pick three of these activities that I could organize that week just to get the ball rolling.

I was going back to KC the next day, and I decided I was going to make three phone calls. I hadn't had a group of friends out to my house to watch a football game for years. I would start making calls to set that up. Earlier in the week I was given the telephone number of a prominent Kansas City Life Coach, Gary Kuzmich. I decided I would call him and set up a meeting. I also decided it was time to plan a trip outside the United States. I couldn't wait to get home.

As the sun set over the Gulf of Mexico that evening, I thought about what a wonderful place Sanibel Island would be to bring a special woman someday. I thought about what a wonderful and exciting life I had and how much I had to share. I knew this was the case before November 12, but it really sank in that early evening. And as I sat in the sand and watched the sun set I also realized I had lived too much of my life within myself. I decided I would really dive into fall and winter volunteer work after I got my personal life squared away. I started to understand that I was relying on other people (a woman) to make me feel good about myself and thus, enjoy life. My friends had been telling me for months how wrong that was. It all sunk in on Sanibel Island. It was time to get back into the game.

New Plans

As I returned to Kansas City from Florida, I spent the entire hour-long drive home from the airport thinking about where I wanted to take my trips. I decided on Jamaica and Rome.

An old friend of mine, Father Gordon Bennett, now lived in Jamaica. I had kept in touch with him since high school and he was always someone I could lean on. I thought this would be a great time to visit him. He could be a great aid toward my recovery.

I had always wanted to visit Rome. I had seen pictures of Vatican City, the ruins, and historic cathedrals. Several friends who had visited Rome told me it was their favorite place in Europe. My friend Kerry Ann was a teacher and would have a break during that time. I was going to invite her to Italy. Kerry Ann and I were once set up on a date but discovered we were better suited as friends and that's how we remained.

As I was driving home from the airport, I passed John Knox Village in Lee's Summit, just a few miles from my house. For years I had passed this retirement home wondering if there was a volunteer opportunity that would appeal to me. It was time for me to stop thinking about, talking about, and researching ways to serve the community during the baseball off-season. No more excuses. Instead of waiting until my personal life was in order before I served the community, how about using community service to help get my personal life in order? I thought about an e-mail my friend Julee had sent me that I had saved, printed, and kept next to my bed. It was the transcript of an interview with Rick Warren, the author of Purpose Driven Life.

"Life is a series of problems: you are in one now, you're just coming out of one, or you're ready to go into another one. The reason for this is that God is more interested in your character than your comfort. God is more interested in making your life holy than He is in making your life happy. And no matter how bad things are in your life, there is always something you can thank God for. You can focus on your purposes, or you can focus on your problems. If you focus on your problems, you're going into self-centeredness, which is 'my problem, my issues, my pain.' But one of the easiest ways to get rid of pain is to get your focus off yourself and onto God and others."

That was it. I had spent so much time focusing on myself and my problems that I had lost sight of my purpose. My problem became my purpose and my purpose became my problem, my issues, and my pain. While I didn't know what caused all of this, the solution somehow became, I wrongly thought, finding a wife. That had become my purpose, to a degree. That's all I wanted to accomplish. It was all about me. I lost my true purpose in life because I was hoping perhaps that someone (a wife) would be the answer and she would somehow rescue me. Not accomplishing this helped fuel the depression. The truth was, nobody was going to come into my life and magically fix me. I needed to fix myself.

I often hear of people who claim they don't have many close friends they can really open up to. Some people don't have one friend like this. Many people have a lot of acquaintances but very few close friends or confidants. The torture of my depression convinced me that I was not only lonely but that I was all alone. The healing of my depression revealed how many close, caring friends I had. It was overwhelming to see and feel the support when my friends and family became aware of my hurt. I was never alone. I just chose to allow myself to feel that way. Perhaps more importantly, I began to listen to and believe what these important people were saying to me and about me.

My depression caused me to feel alone and useless. Not only did I lose sight of how many great friends I had, I had forgotten what a great friend I had been to them

– another of the many side effects of depression. Friends have often told me since about the many times I was there for them. I also remembered that one of the few things that brought me a speck of light in my darkness was helping a friend in need. It took the focus off me and onto another, as Rick Warren suggested. It also gave me a temporary feeling of joy because I was helping someone else. I started to understand that helping others helped me.

I wasn't going to spend another off-season checking my voice mail and email 25 times a day waiting for someone to call me and rescue me from my loneliness. What a waste of time. I was still taking life one foot in front of the other, but now my strides were getting longer.

John Knox

There were many different components to my recovery. Some were obvious: therapy with Dale, support of friends and family, and, of course, the medication, which helped correct a chemical imbalance. Perhaps the less obvious component was equally as important: volunteer work.

Any specialist helping a person deal with Major Depressive Disorder would agree that recovery first begins with the afflicted acknowledging his or her problem. There is a major difference between just being told you have a problem and actually accepting and feeling that a problem exists. One must have an acknowledgement of the problem. Recovery is sped along when the afflicted takes the time to deal with the issues that led up to MDD. There comes a time when the sufferer can no longer avoid the problem and must accept the fact that they need medication and psychotherapy. These two steps aren't theory. They are essential. Both steps were critical in my journey and my recovery. I discovered what was triggering my anxiety (through therapy), how to control the condition (medication), and how to move forward (a life coach). But I was also looking for a new purpose.

I started my search for purpose by focusing on others. There is a variable amount of time that must be taken to deal with the issues that lead to MDD but it is important eventually to own the pain and move on. For me, a part of moving on was through community service. As mentioned earlier, the only time I was able to experience relief during the depths of MDD was to focus on my family and friends and their problems. I still don't know if a loss of hope caused my condition or my condition caused me to experience a loss of hope. Nevertheless, loss of hope was at the core. Attempting to restore my friends and family gave me some second-hand hope that I was able to inhale and use as fuel for a short period of time. So as I looked for a way to strengthen that hope, I searched for opportunities where I might be able to give to those who were short on hope or were actually hopeless.

I hosted my first Bible Study for a group from the local high school on November 28. I saw it as an opportunity to share my faith, but it was also an enormous responsibility because of how impressionable high school kids are. I was nervous and ecstatic at the same time. Eight kids showed up the first night. I put together a study sheet for our first night's lesson and, after eating some pizza, we went down into my basement and went to work. I got the discussion started but the kids gave it life. I was awed by the depth of the kids and their willingness to share. The kids and I traded hope that first night and in the following weeks. That was just the beginning.

John Knox Village provides a community for several stages of elderly life (independent living, assisted living, nursing home care, Alzheimer's Care, and hospice care). Knowing how my own widowed grandmothers enjoy company, I decided to stop by John Knox to see what volunteer opportunities were available.

It was decided that I would split my time between visiting residents in the nursing home, visiting patients at Lee's Summit Hospital in conjunction with John Knox's chaplain office, and visiting infants at the employee child care center. I had no idea what was ahead of me.

My original plan was to donate my time to people who might need a visitor and some comfort. I figured I would spend some time with the elderly at the nursing home and hospital by simply listening to their life stories and concerns. What I ended up with was more valuable therapy for me, as well as some invaluable lessons about life.

The first person that had an impact on me at John Knox village was Duane Wise. Duane was a 79-year-old independent living resident, a widower of three years, and a volunteer chaplain. Duane told me about his life's triumphs and tribulations. He talked about becoming a successful sporting goods store owner and about his late wife. He talked about his faith and how he ministered to prisoners for several years at state and federal penitentiaries in nearby Leavenworth, Kansas. I walked away with a thought-provoking lesson about men's behavior: When Duane talked about something emotional, tears ran down his face. He wiped away the tears with no shame. When he reflected on something humorous, he unleashed a healthy laugh. When he wasn't sure about one of my questions, he took the time to stop and think.

All of his answers seemed genuine.

Two days later I volunteered at the child care center. There were six babies under the age of 12 months that day under the supervision of two child-care workers (and me, sort of). It wasn't easy. Infants, obviously, need constant care. In the first two hours, I think I saw each child cry, laugh, or look totally confused as they tried to figure out some sort of toy.

I was struck by how pure Duane's and the infants' emotions were. Seventy-nine years separated these generations yet when it was time to cry, each generation cried. When they were compelled to laugh, they laughed.

When a situation that required thought presented itself, they thought before responding. So much happens to us between infancy and retirement. We come into the world vulnerable and we leave the world the same. I thought about Jim Valvano's famous speech at the 1993 ESPY Awards as he received the Arthur Ashe Courage Award. The former national champion college basketball coach is most remembered for his, "Don't give up, don't ever give up" message that night in front of a national television audience 55 days before losing his life to bone marrow cancer. For some reason, I always remembered another portion of that speech:

"Now, I'm fighting cancer, everybody knows that. People ask me all the time about how you go through your life and how's your day, and nothing is changed for me. As Dick (Vitale) said, I'm a very emotional, passionate man. I can't help it. That's being the son of Rocco and Angelina Valvano. It comes with the territory. We hug, we kiss, we love. And when people say to me how do you get through life or each day, it's the same thing. To me, there are three things we all should do every day. We should do this every day of our lives. Number one is laugh. You should laugh every day. Number two is think. You should spend some time in thought. And number three is, you should have your emotions moved to tears, could be happiness or joy. But think about it. If you laugh, you think, and you cry, that's a full day. That's a heck of a day. You do that seven days a week, you're going to have something special."

In my first week at John Knox Village I also visited patients at Lee's Summit Hospital. This was another unforgettable experience. Members of the chaplain's office make weekly visits to John Knox residents who are hospitalized. The chaplains offer spiritual support and comfort and do an admirable job of handling patients of varying mental, emotional, and physical states. Some of the patients were very willing and easy to visit with. Other patients were confused about why they were in the hospital and when they were going home. And some were so ill or medicated they were unable to communicate (verbally or otherwise). At first this experience was quite uncomfortable and it would take several visits to understand that I was there to do whatever I could to make them, not me, comfortable.

At about the same time, I started visiting residents at the John Knox Village nursing home. A program was designed for volunteers to spend time with men and women who were unable to participate in group activities or who didn't get many visitors. I was first paired up with 93-year-old Harold Bartley, a former elementary school principal from a small town in northeastern Kansas. Mr. Bartley had suffered a few strokes and was mostly confined to his bed or a wheelchair. His speech was slurred, but his mind was very sharp. His wife, Bevie, lived in the room next door but was dealing with the onset of Alzheimer's disease. Harold and Bevie had meals together but were no longer able to share a room. Before retirement they spent their summers traveling the world. He loved ice cream and we visited the care center's ice cream parlor for dessert and a chat. Harold served four years in the Air Force during World War II in Hawaii. Luckily for him, he didn't get his orders to report there until after the attack on Pearl Harbor in 1941. But he did see the damage it left behind.

While making a hospital visit one week, I met 90-year-old Sarah McMillan. Sarah was going to be released from the hospital soon and was returning to the care center. As I was preparing to leave, I told Sarah I would visit her at the Care Center when she was released from the hospital. Sarah explained that nobody visited her anymore, a thought that saddened me.

I visited Sarah several times and quickly developed a nice friendship with her. She is originally from Scotland and still carries the distinctive accent. She was a nurse in England during World War II when she met an American GI and moved to the United States. As a nurse in England, Sarah had responsibilities not unlike American doctors. She wrote prescriptions and delivered babies. One year during the war, she delivered 280 babies.

I learned a lot about life during the war from Harold and Sarah and others, but I had to ask about it. I also learned quite a bit about their career accomplishments, but I had to ask about that as well. What I learned the most about Harold, Sarah, and the many people I visited at the hospital that off-season surprised me. Unlike my generation, there wasn't much free discussion about careers, salaries, cars, and personal accomplishments. Instead, by and large, the people I visited talked more about their families. They talked about what their children and grandchildren had accomplished. They talked about the houses they had lived in for 40-50 years. They talked about missing their friends in the neighborhood. They talked about their flower and vegetable gardens. They talked about places they had visited and people they had met. They talked about their churches. When they recalled a sad moment, they shed a tear. If they remembered something funny, they laughed. When I asked them a question, they took the time to stop and think before answering.

Volunteering at John Knox Village taught me how important relationships are. The residents at John Knox

Village and patients at Lee's Summit Hospital reminded me that we're not really going anywhere in life when we only focus on ourselves. Relationships are about doing things for each other; living for each other. A nurse told me the happiest residents at the nursing home are always the ones who get the most visitors.

With hope, we feel like we can achieve anything. Without hope, life has little meaning.

A new appreciation came to light thanks to my experience at John Knox and Lee's Summit Hospital. What we all need to survive is something I once had in great abundance yet almost completely lost in the summer of 2005 – hope, the hope of friendships, the hope of relationships, the hope of greater meaning. My recovery gained much momentum when I was able to pass that hope on to others who had lost it. With hope, we feel like we can achieve anything. Without hope, life has little meaning.

Gary

Because of busy schedules followed by Thanksgiving, Life Coach Gary Kuzmich and I weren't able to meet until November 29. Gary was advertised as someone who could complement my therapy with Dale and literally coach me through my quest to rediscover my purpose. By the time our meeting date arrived I was feeling very good about where I was headed. I had begun volunteering at John Knox and at the hospital. I was spending time with family and friends. I had a trip planned to Italy. And I was hungry for more. It didn't take long for Gary to convince me that I could go much further.

When we first met, Gary was a hip looking, 53-year-old former professional freestyle skier who could pass as actor George Hamilton's son. After severe injuries to a shoulder and hip, he became a professional ski instructor and world class freestyle coach. From there he became an ordained minister, a professional musician, a vice president at John Hancock Insurance and Financial Services, a corporate marketing consultant, and eventually the successful owner of his own financial services company. His real passion, however, was his Life Coach business.

Just nine years earlier, Gary found himself in a situation not unlike mine. He was 44 years old and was dealing with a divorce and a failed business that left him lying on his bed one night in the fetal position, crying uncontrollably. He was dealing with his perceived present failures, and, evidently, some buried feelings of isolation, abandonment, and betrayal. Like me, he had suppressed those feelings for many years and was able to hide behind the façade of a happy face. He referred to it as his mask. But eventually he lost the ability to overpower his pain. Suddenly, he had to deal directly with it. My emotional crash occurred at an earlier age and under different circumstances, but my plight was very much like Gary's.

We met for lunch. After exchanging the usual first-meeting pleasantries, we sat down. Almost immediately, Gary launched into action.

"So, who are you pissed off at?" he asked.

"Who am I pissed of at?" I said, startled. "I don't think I'm pissed off at anyone."

"OK, then what are you ashamed of?"

"Ashamed of? Well, I'm ashamed of many things but I don't think it has anything to do with why I'm here."

"What are you afraid of?"

"I guess I'm afraid of being alone."

"You guess?"

"Yeah, I…well…no, I am afraid of being alone."

"Why are you afraid of being alone?"

"I don't know, because I…"

"What do you mean, you don't know? You know why you are afraid to be alone. Either you don't want to tell me or you're ashamed of why you are afraid of being alone."

"I don't mind telling you."

"Then your hesitation means you are ashamed of why you are afraid of being alone. Is that why you're here?"

"I guess that's part of it."

"But you just told me that shame has nothing to do with why you're here."

Less than two minutes into our first session I knew Gary was my kind of guy. He went on to explain that while anxiety and depression can be perpetuated by a chemical reaction in the brain, there is almost always a catalyst. This precipitating event triggers the brain's reaction to the event. He explained that the catalyst is the result of one or more deeply embedded emotions: unresolved anger, shame, or fear. In my case, and in most cases, anger, fear, and shame work together if the original emotion is buried. Like a chain reaction, one ignored emotion gives life to another emotion which breaths life into yet another emotion.

I explained the successful work I had done with Dale that revealed my previously undetected detachment from my mother.

"I guess I have been ashamed of the emotional detachment from my mother," I said.

"Why have you been ashamed?"

"Because I don't know how a woman would handle a man who has some emotional voids in his life. I haven't had a very good experience with sharing my needs and voids."

"So you are afraid of what a woman might think of you being a sensitive man with feelings?"

"I don't know if I'm afraid of it..."

"So then you are comfortable telling a woman, 'I am a sensitive man with feelings.' "

"Well, I don't know if I would come right out and say that on the first date."

"Why not? Isn't that who you are?"

"Yeah, but not everyone wants to hear that."

"No, you're right. Not everyone wants to hear that. But some people do. What if a woman told you she was a sensitive person with feelings? Would that make you uncomfortable?"

"No."

"OK, what if a buddy of yours admitted he was a sensitive man with feelings. Would that make you think any less of him?"

"No, I would think that was pretty brave of him."

"OK, let me get all of this straight. You would think a buddy of yours would be very brave to admit he was sensitive with feelings. But it's not OK for you to share this about yourself with others?"

"I could probably share that with...not probably...I could share that about myself with someone who was like-minded."

"Do you believe you are the only person who is sensitive with feelings?"

"Of course not. I'm sure many people feel the same way I do."

"Has it crossed your mind that you might be choosing people in relationships who are afraid of finding out about themselves what you've found out about yourself?"

Gary explained to me that everyone has feelings, needs, and voids. People who appear to be emotionless are usually the people who have been hurt the most. They have been taught by someone else or by their own misguided intuition to ignore their emotions. These people are the most afraid. They are also the most imprisoned because they will not allow themselves to feel anything, including happiness.

Gary also explained that we tend to look at those who are unhappy all of the time as the only legitimate people with an emotional disorder. But it isn't possible to be forever unhappy unless a person chooses to place themselves physically and emotionally in that environment. In order to rediscover happiness, you have to deal with the unhappiness and most people don't want to go there. The same is true with people who appear to be happy all of the time. It is naturally impossible to be happy all of the time yet some people strive to convince themselves and others that it is realistically possible. This made me think of the people I have known who have a reputation of being cheerful every minute of every day. When I got to know these people on a deeply personal level, I was surprised to learn of all the pain they've had to endure in their lifetimes. Choosing to keep people at a distance by being happy all of the time is no different than putting up a wall by being somber all of the time. In most cases, the cure is much more frightening than the ailment.

Gary also helped me redefine a word.

"When I use the word 'vulnerable' what comes to mind?" he asked.

"I don't know. I guess the word has a 'weakness' connotation to it."

"What does it mean to you?"

"I think it means that the person has been broken down and is somewhat emotional."

"What do you mean by broken down?"

"I'm thinking of someone who has had something difficult happen in their lives and they have broken down and become emotional."

"But what has broken down? Something had to be built up to be broken down."

"I don't know. Some sort of wall of defense."

"That's exactly what it is."

My discussions with Gary made me realize that my perception of the word "vulnerable" was misguided, and that being vulnerable can be a good thing. We are mostly on guard to never let ourselves be vulnerable. We protect our hearts as if we are at war in our social lives. Even in our closest relationships we act as though we are at war and we build layers and layers of walls around our hearts and invite people to come right up to the exterior of the wall but no closer. By having this war-like attitude, we enter into relationships with people we never really get to know. These relationships may become intimate on a physical level but fail to become intimate on an emotional level.

As Gary and I looked back on some of my recent romantic relationships, it was clear that the level of intimacy didn't grow much past the physical side. There was very little depth on the emotional side. By avoiding the emotional side, these relationships became rooted and dependent on physical intimacy and eventually ended. I became attracted to people who didn't ask me who I was, and I attracted people who didn't want to tell me who they were.

Gary also explained intimacy in a way I had never considered. He said everyone is born with a need for intimacy. Intimacy, he said, is a need to let others know you. Think of your closest friendships: Why are they so strong? It's because they know you.

Yet I know I created relationships with people who were also fearful of being intimate. I didn't really know who they were, and they didn't know who I was. But the need for intimacy didn't disappear. By suppressing my need for emotional intimacy and using sexual intimacy as my only means of being known, I never gained the benefits of a true romantic relationship.

In reference to my work with Dale and discovering my

emotional detachment from my mother, Gary explained that my journey, in his opinion, was a reclamation of my childhood.

"Who did God originally intend you to be?" he asked.

"What are the true desires of your heart?"

"Who were you before you experienced the pain of detachment?"

"Who would you have been had you not used alcohol and drugs that put you in a state of mind other than your own?"

I stayed silent. But I was excited and motivated to find the answers. Then, Gary had a question waiting for me that would become the defining theme of my breakdown and the catalyst of my path to recovery.

"Is Ryan enough?"

Jamaica

I had been looking forward to spending time with Fr. Bennett ever since walking on the beach of Sanibel Island. For the past 20 years, he has been my "spiritual guru." I have met many people who have inspired me and lifted my spirits over that time span, but nobody centers me like Fr. Bennett. I landed in Kingston, Jamaica, at 8 PM on December 10. Fr. Bennett had sent a driver for me, and when I arrived at his home in Mandeville, he opened his back door and greeted me with a hearty hug.

Fr. Bennett was now 59 but he still looked the same to me as when I first met him 20 years ago as a freshman at Loyola High School in Los Angeles. A 5'6" African-American, I never felt any difference in race or culture with him from the very first day I heard him speak.

Fr. Bennett delivered the homily at the first Mass I ever attended at Loyola High School and it was the first time I remember being moved by a person of religious office. He has a wonderful sense of humor and has remained relatively contemporary through the years. He is comforting yet challenging. He is also one of the wisest and most compassionate people I have ever met. Beginning his eighth year as bishop in the church, his official titles are Bishop Bennett, Most Reverend Bennett, and His Lordship. Still, to me, he will always be Father Bennett. I think he likes that I still refer to the title he held when he was just a priest.

It is very rare for me not to share serious events in my life with Fr. Bennett. Yet I didn't communicate with him at all during the summer. When I emailed earlier and asked if I could visit him, I simply shared that some amazing things had been happening in my life and that I needed some navigation. After I got to Jamaica, it didn't take us long to dive into serious matters.

"So," Fr. Bennett said before taking a deep breath, "tell me. How is your life?"

I presented a synopsis summary of 2005 from August 7 right up to pulling into his driveway. I must have rambled on for 30 minutes.

"My goodness, you've had quite a year," he said. "How do you feel?"

"I feel much better now. As the days go by I understand why I needed to go through this and get through this."

"Why do you believe you needed to go through this and get through it? Do you think God put you through this intentionally?"

"I think He allowed me to go through it."

"But why did He allow you to go through it?"

"Because I needed to?"

"But how did He know you needed to?"

"Well, He knew because He knows the desires of my heart better than I do."

"That's right but how else did He know? Because you asked Him to. You said a while earlier that God answered your prayer. Your prayer is nothing more than going to the Father and telling Him what you desire. He wants to give you your heart's desire but He wants to hear it from you, first. By hearing it from your mouth, He is allowing you to tell Him and yourself what it is you desire. Then it's up to Him to use His grace to answer your prayer."

"So this is where free will comes into play?"

"Free will...yes. I believe people don't understand the freedom God gives us. He loves us but He also sets us free. You asked Him to be purified and to help you resolve your incompleteness. He answered your prayer but you accepted the suffering that came with it. Not everyone endures the suffering. They ignore it and go back to their own ways. That's one of the great mysteries of suffering; to actually accept it. That's also free will, Ryan."

At first, I was blown away by this. My suffering was partly a result of my own free will? Then I began to remember all of the times in my life when I chose to medicate myself with alcohol and drugs instead of dealing with the suffering.

"Ryan, this also extends into finding a wife," he continued. "Free will applies to all of the relationships we develop."

"Doesn't God put the right people in our lives?"

"Free will allows everyone to come into your life. God just wants to be part of the decision-making process. You see, there are people that you desire in your life, but is God part of your decision or is it your own desire? There are also people you avoid for obvious reasons; you don't even think twice. Other people also have free will to allow you to come into their lives. Are we using God to help us decide? That's the question."

"So I have a much bigger role in my fate than I thought."

"You do. You have free will. But remember, God is

always trying to communicate with us. In some way, He is always telling us something. We, with our free will, have to be willing to listen. I tell people that the God-phone is always ringing. We just allow the static and noise of the world to distract us from the call."

With that Fr. Bennett reminded me that a man of his age doesn't usually stay up until midnight and it was time to get to sleep.

The next morning, we were right back at it.

"Ryan, I'm curious. Have you truly reconciled your feeling of abandonment?" he asked.

"Well, I know what has caused my pain. I know why I have pursued what I have pursued my entire life."

"Has it changed the way you feel about yourself today?"

"I think I recognize what gets me into trouble. I think I can better identify what is a healthy and unhealthy relationship. I think I'm much less afraid of being abandoned."

"But does it change the way you feel about yourself?"

"Yeah. I realize I wasn't ever abandoned. I just felt a detachment from my Mom. I don't feel that way now and I think this will help me move forward."

"What did that detachment cause you to do?"

"It caused me to seek attachment from women like

my Mom. Or at least the vision I had of her when I was very young. I have met some wonderful women in my life but, if they didn't fulfill the void left by my detachment, I moved on. I was searching for something but I didn't know what it was. In the meantime I was sabotaging myself along the way."

"So there was a pattern? Describe it for me."

"OK. I would see a woman I was attracted to. Like other males in the room, I would immediately seek validation for myself by trying to attract her to me. I think I felt that way with my Mom when I was young, too."

"You were competing for her love and attention."

"Yes. At least that's the way I felt. So I would pursue this woman I was attracted to and sometimes she would respond. Then we would become an item and I would feel like I had fulfilled this void in my life. But then I would sense that when I was with her, she would still desire attention from others. But all I wanted was to have her to myself. But I felt that it wasn't enough for her."

"Yes, and you were back to competing for her love and attention, just like with your Mom."

I saw how it all fit together, the pattern of my behavior. This was different than my therapy with Dale, though just as helpful. And that is how I spent my three days in Jamaica, just talking and sharing philosophy with

Fr. Bennett. We'd talk, we'd eat, we'd talk some more, and we'd talk even more until it was time to sleep. It was spiritual therapy, at least in my mind. I had numerous breakthroughs during my visit with Fr. Bennett, far too numerous to list in one chapter or perhaps even one book. As I thought I would, I felt so much more centered as I was set to leave Jamaica.

Interestingly, as I arrived at the airport, two women there asked me to fill out a survey for the Jamaican Tourist Board. I tried to explain that I didn't visit any beaches or any restaurants or any music festivals. I didn't do any of the traditional tourist things. But I had a great time nonetheless. They seem puzzled but they didn't seem to mind. I certainly didn't mind, either.

Rome

Kerry Ann, who was a sweet friend and great to pal around with, and I began our long trip to Rome, Italy, on December 17. Our first day consisted of a one-hour drive to the airport, a one-hour flight to Minneapolis, a seven and-a-half hour flight to Amsterdam, a three-hour layover, and a 90-minute flight into Rome. I had traveled quite a bit through the years with the Twins and the Royals but that was domestic traveling. Kerry Ann was much more seasoned in this type of travel, so she became the official coordinator. It was her job to plan the day and get us to our destinations through the tangled streets of Rome. Our first day was December 18. Our first stop was the famous Spanish Steps.

On the walk there, I noticed that Rome seemed to be filled with couples. Men and women of all ages walked together arm and arm. Kerry Ann and I were just friends but I thought, "When in Rome…" Being the gentleman that I am, I offered my arm to Kerry Ann.

"No thanks, I'm good," she said, smiling.

With that, our seven and-a-half day trip began.

It was a sunny afternoon with the temperature in the 50s. For two people from the Midwest escaping winter, this seemed fine. For the locals, it was cold. Most everyone was bundled up in big coats, gloves, scarves, and hats. Every street corner had a vendor selling roasted chestnuts. The aroma was fantastic. Having never tasted roasted chestnuts, I ordered a bag. Well, now I know why in The Christmas Song, the writer refers to "chestnuts roasting on an open fire" but never mentions anyone actually eating chestnuts. I couldn't stand them.

I saw everything I wanted to see in Rome, some places more than once. I was fascinated by the history. Standing inside the Roman Colosseum and walking through the Forum and Pantheon were unforgettable experiences. The most awe inspiring part of the trip for me was St. Peter's Square and Basilica at Vatican City.

It was the first place I have visited in my life that was actually bigger in person than it looked on television. It was massive and strikingly beautiful.

While in Rome, I didn't spend much time thinking about the pain I had endured earlier in the year or where I was on my journey. I was able to put it all aside and just enjoyed the trip. But I did have a powerful experience inside St. Peter's that helped me understand and have peace with my struggle.

Upon entering the magnificent basilica I noticed a group of people surrounding a piece of art. There were several thousand people scattered inside St. Peter's taking in the artistic brilliance of every corner. But the largest gathering huddled in one corner, taking pictures of a sculpture. As I approached I recognized the flawless work of Michelangelo's *Pieta*. Most Catholic churches (especially cathedrals and basilicas) have a chapel or place of honor for devotion to the Virgin Mary. In the most famous of all basilicas in the world, St. Peter's used the life-sized, marble portrayal of Mary holding the body of her son after His death.

I studied this image for quite some time. I just kept looking at the portrayal of Mary holding her son. And then I started to think about my own situation. Even though I had learned that the pain men suffer due to an emotional detachment from their mother is very

> I'm sure most people staring at this famous Christian artwork saw a graceful religious symbol of the Son of God and the Mother of the Church. I simply saw a mother and her son.

real and very common, I truly wondered if my story would be powerful enough to strike a chord in the hearts of others. I wondered if my story was masculine enough. Recovery stories that deal with an overbearing father – those strike chords with many people. Overcoming an addiction to alcohol and drugs – those do, too. Even addictions to sex and pornography have become recognizable disorders that need to be addressed and treated. But reconciling a detachment from your mother – to some, it's just not manly. Then I looked at Mary and her son again – He would become the most painted, sculpted, and studied person in the history of mankind. His story changed the world forever. And here He was, in the place where His life began, in the arms of His mother. Soon He would be laid to rest in a tomb and would rise again as the savior of the world to many. But for now, His lifeless body was held only by Mom. I imagined Him as a little boy, safe and secure with his mother. And now, in this portrayal, He was there again, in mother's arms. I'm sure most people staring at this famous Christian artwork saw a graceful religious symbol of the Son of God and the Mother of the Church. I simply saw a mother and her son.

We continued our tour through St. Peter's and stopped to pray in the Chapel of the Blessed Sacrament. It is a chapel by name only; it's as big as many American churches. As we knelt and faced the altar, I was awestruck by how many different people from different countries were doing exactly what I was doing. I had a hard time praying for my own intentions and the intentions of others in my life. Instead, I just looked around the chapel and tried to imagine what my worldly brothers and sisters were praying for. I had come so far in the past four months thanks to available modern medicine and psychotherapy. I never took the time to consider that most people in the world don't have the finances or the access to the things that we take for granted in the United States. So many countries were represented in that chapel by different gender, culture, skin color, and facial expression. Yet we all had one thing in common. We were all openly displaying our human limits by presenting our fears, struggles, victories, joys, and pains before God.

Our tour continued to St. Peter's grotto, the final resting place for several popes, including the recently deceased John Paul II. The most powerful sight, for me, in the St. Peter grotto was the final resting place of the basilica's namesake. Directly beneath the majestic dome and main altar lay the remains of the apostle Peter, a man who walked with Jesus and eventually was given the assignment to establish the church after Christ was crucified. The Catholic Church considers Peter its first pope.

Four days later we would watch Pope Benedict XVI – 1,938 years after St. Peter – preside over his first midnight Mass on Christmas Eve in front of thousands in attendance and millions on worldwide television as the 265th pope in church history. The Mass was spoken primarily in Latin and Italian but also included English, French, Dutch, German, Swahili, Filipino, Polish, Portuguese, Hebrew, and Spanish. Children from all over the world presented the pope with communion bread and wine. It was a fascinating event, both spiritually and culturally.

My visit to Rome turned out better than I could have imagined, and left lasting impressions on me, like the one of a son resting in his mother's arms.

Focus

Part of my coaching with Gary Kuzmich included participating in Focus, a Kansas City-based, personal-effectiveness seminar owned by Wayne and Pam McKamie. Gary was a graduate of the seminar and eventually became part of the training staff. He and Wayne had co-authored a book together, The Passionate Heroic Zone. I trusted Gary, as our sessions were excitingly productive. The year 2006 had arrived and I was feeling much healthier physically and emotionally and looked forward to any device that would help make the new year better than 2005. Plus, I have always had an interest in human behavior (through good times and bad) so there was no resistance on my part about attending Focus.

I arrived at the Focus building on January 6, 2006, feeling a little nervous about embarking on an unfamiliar journey but mostly excited about carrying my momentum to a new level. I had a much better understanding and acceptance of who I was, and I was coming to realize that Ryan was enough. I began the early stages of chronicling my experiences for this book and I found that it was providing valuable therapy – I had found another way to express myself from the heart. Five months after my breakdown on August 7, I also was beginning to share my experience with people who had been otherwise outside my inner circle. Yet there was still more for me.

It's hard to describe something as one of the greatest experiences of your life without explaining how or why, but that's about all you will get out of a Focus graduate. For one, this personal experience is difficult to put into words. Second, it's a rule that you don't share details of the process because it would ruin the experience for someone who might choose to participate. What I can share is that Focus helped each one of us break down the walls surrounding our hearts. I say help because nobody ever told me who I was; I discovered it on my own. As Wayne puts it, "Focus isn't an outward-in process, it's an inward-out process." In other words, the answers are already inside of us. We just need the tools and the courage to dig those answers out. Living from the heart isn't easy, but once it has been achieved there is no other way to live.

As Wayne began his presentation, I was hooked after his first Focus principle: Getting rid of the argument of Right versus Wrong and replacing it with Working versus Not Working.

I have spent a great deal of my emotional energy evaluating and over-analyzing every detail of my life. Romantic relationships are right at the top of the list, but I have also beaten my brain to a pulp by dissecting close friendships, casual friendships, family relationships, work relationships, and spiritual relationships. I have also wasted most of this time because I focused too much on who is right in these relationships and who is wrong. Sometimes it was analyzing whether the relationship itself was right or wrong. I would classify my behavior or another's behavior as justified (right) or unjustified (wrong). Like most people I was more concerned with my reputation than the strength of the relationship. Therefore, I would think even harder to create ways where I was nearly always right and rarely wrong. Until the first night of Focus, I had no idea there was a better and more fulfilling way to go about this.

What would it look like if I threw ego to the wind and asked myself one question regarding my behavior, relationships, and environment: Is this working or not working? Forget about who's right and who's wrong. Is it working or not working? That is a simple question to answer. After you've gone this far, ask yourself, "Why isn't this working? What are the reasons this particular situation doesn't work?" And then ask yourself, "What is working? Are there facets of my situation that are working, as few as there may be? Can I build on what's working? Can I communicate my concerns with the other party?" If the answer is no, then get back to the first question: Is this working or not working? This was simple, yet fascinating stuff for me.

By applying the inside-out approach, Focus allowed

me to discover, for myself, the true desires of my heart. I believe we are all wired uniquely. Around the age of 4, I began to believe that I wasn't enough. That was the beginning of the "construction era" of my life. I began building walls around my wounded heart. Life operated on the outside of the walls in the form of an image. On the inside of the walls was a wounded inner child who wasn't allowed to grieve. Instead, he was silenced. In *Homecoming: Reclaiming and Championing Your Inner Child*, author John Bradshaw describes how silencing our wounded inner child is an act of sabotaging ourselves:

"When we are unable to grieve, we cannot finish the past. All the emotional energy relating to our distress or trauma becomes frozen. Unresolved and unexpressed, this energy continually tries to resolve itself. Since it cannot be expressed in healthy grieving, it is expressed in abnormal behavior."

After 30 years of abnormal behavior (construction), life clearly wasn't working for me. Focus helped me plow through my walls and allowed me to get back to the man God designed me to be so that I could begin living my life instead of the image I had chosen and others had chosen for me. One of the best examples of knocking down these walls is a scene from the movie *Good Will Hunting.* Matt Damon's character, Will Hunting, a closed-off, tough man, had made very little progress in his therapy sessions with Robin Williams' character, Sean. After concentrating on Will's present-day attitude for several meetings, Williams decided to plow through the thick walls around his patient's heart and speak to the wounded inner child. The "It's not your fault" scene is the most memorable in the movie to me, and is a powerful example of un-layering.

In case you never saw the movie, in their last session, Sean holds a folder in his hand that contains Will's file from social services. The folder contains reports and diagnoses from other therapists as well as graphic photographs of the physical abuse Will suffered as a child at the hands of his foster father. Sean holds the folder out in front of Will's face and tells him, "It's not your fault." It's obvious that Will has heard this before and he responds with a condescending eye-roll and says, "I know." Will's defenses are thick and sturdy and this comment from Sean bounces off his patient's emotional walls without a dent. This is where most people in Will's life quit on him. Sean takes a step closer, "Look at me son, it's not your fault." He attempts to speak to Will's wounded inner child by calling him son. Again, Will brushes this comment aside and responds, "I know."

Yet, he also turns and looks away in an attempt to avoid Sean. Sean continues, "It's not your fault." Will recognizes that casually blowing off Sean's good intentions isn't driving him away, so Will goes on the offensive and says "I know" in a sarcastic tone. Sean, undaunted, takes a step closer to Will and repeats, "It's not your fault." Will is now becoming uncomfortable because for the first time he hasn't been able to drive someone away. He stands up and tries to walk away. Sean gets closer and prevents Will's escape. Sean repeats, "It's not your fault." Will stops. Sean has made a connection.

Like the faint sound of a child trapped beneath the rubble of a fallen building, Sean can hear Will's wounded inner child pleading for help. Sean stays at it, "It's not your fault." Tears begin to run down Will's face. "It's not your fault," Sean says again. In a last ditch effort to protect his wounded inner child, Will turns to anger and gives Sean a threatening look. Sean takes another step towards Will, "It's not your fault." Will has become vulnerable and it doesn't feel good. Fear sets in. His anger walls are crumbling and fear causes him to push Sean away. Will has used fear to push people away from him, literally and figuratively, to protect his wounded inner child for years. He is a tough guy. Sean isn't intimated. He knows he is close and says again, "It's not your fault." Will's anger walls of defense have been dismantled. His wounded inner child is exposed. Now Sean has the responsibility of comforting a child that has been lost in the emotional rubble for many years. He has successfully plowed through the thick walls surrounding Will's heart but his work is far from complete. How he accepts and receives this child will play a vital role in how Will Hunting will accept and receive his own inner child. Sean, like the comforting father Will never had, steps closer. He wraps his right hand behind Will's head, stroking his hair gently and whispers, "It's not your fault." Will cannot silence his inner child any longer. He embraces Sean tightly and allows his inner child to grieve for the first time. As he accepts love and comfort from a father figure for the first time in his life, Will says through his sobs, "I'm sorry. I'm so sorry." Sean was right all along, Will's wounded inner child did believe the abuse was the result of his own doing. What Will Hunting needed all of his life was his wounded inner child to be embraced and loved.

Dale Williamson, Gary Kuzmich, my mother, and Focus reintroduced me to my wounded inner child and allowed him to be embraced. Not only was he embraced but he began to live. And my inner child taught me a lot about myself.

This process led to the most important lesson I took from my Focus experience. As I was realizing the deepest desires of my heart and living solely from my heart, I was able to see others in the Focus group experience the same. I witnessed 40 other people move to demolish their protective walls and return to their inner child. It amazed me that while we had different life experiences, we all had similar emotional issues. In some degree or another, we all lived our lives believing that we were not enough. On the other side of the façade was a child who was wounded and silenced. Once I began to view the others in the group through these new lenses, my judgments were gone. Our wounded inner children were set free and able to interact the way innocent, joyful children interact. It didn't matter what circumstances life had thrown our way, the color of our skin, whether we were male or female, or how much money we had. We simply accepted each other the way we were. It wasn't a judgmental image that did the talking, it was the unconditionally loving child inside of us.

This was a huge discovery for me because I spent my entire life judging relationships based on my life experience. My life was complex and people had to understand that. When a romantic relationship began to sour, I chalked it up to her not understanding where I was coming from. It was all about me and my wounded inner child. My experience with Focus blessed me with a newfound capability to be sympathetic to the wounded inner child inside of someone else and their struggle to live up to believing they weren't enough. I became a better listener by allowing my inner child to reach out to someone else's inner child and allow those children to feel safe with one another. Knowing the deepest desires of someone else's heart is much more interesting to me than their stories of achievement and accumulation. By sharing my heart, I made it safer for those around me to share theirs. The walls around my heart were replaced by bridges, connecting my inner child's heart to the heart of my friends' inner child.

Shame of Man

After I was properly diagnosed and began taking an anti-depressant back in August, I did some research on anxiety and Major Depressive Disorder. I found that research reveals that women are twice as likely to suffer from these conditions as men. I also discovered that women are four times more likely to utilize psychotherapy than men. There are numerous theories on why the latter is true, but I believe women are simply more willing to admit they are depressed and take some action. A big part of dealing with depression is dealing with emotions and insecurities. Most women seem to have an edge over men in terms of examining their feelings. Men, however, are four times more likely to abuse alcohol and drugs. Men are more likely to use tobacco as a habit than are women. Men are more addicted to pornography and gambling than women by an astronomical difference. There is no comparison in the percentage of violence committed by men as opposed to women. Men are more likely to be labeled a workaholic.

So both sexes are vulnerable to emotional disorders such as depression, but women are more likely to address the problem directly and medicate the problem directly. Men are less likely to address the problem directly and will medicate the problem indirectly with alcohol, illegal drugs, smoking, pornography, gambling, and by overworking. Or worse, they will not be able to medicate themselves and some turn to violence. I also suspect that women suffer from depression and seek psychotherapy at a much higher rate than men because they have to deal not only with their own issues but also the issues of stubborn men who won't seek help.

Suppressing and repressing these issues is a debilitating and confusing experience for men. The options become: Address the issues head-on with psychotherapy and/or modern medicines that are designed to treat these disorders, or run away from the actual problems and use other forms of medication to make the emotional pain go away. Perhaps not coincidentally, men also commit suicide at a much higher rate than women. It's not hard to draw the conclusion that many men may wind up committing suicide because they try too hard to avoid the pain, rather than accepting it and combating it. John Bradshaw wrote:

"The brain has no trouble with life's occasional distress. It uses the expression of emotion to maintain balance. When our distress reaches a certain peak, we storm with anger, weep with sadness, or perspire and tremble with fear. Scientists have shown that tears actually remove stressful chemicals that build up during emotional upset. The brain will be naturally moved to equilibrium by means of the expression of emotion unless we are taught to inhibit it."

Thankfully, I realized that being depressed didn't mean that I wasn't tough enough, and eventually I got help. Admitting a problem and doing something about it means you are brave enough. I remember thinking, "If I'm on medication for depression, something must really be wrong with me." Well, something was really wrong with me. It had nothing to do with how old I was, how healthy I was, or how successful I was. Depression doesn't profile or discriminate. It doesn't care who or what you are. It doesn't matter how strong you think you are. If you're one of the unfortunate, it will get you. But there is a way out.

For most men, having the courage to seek medical attention (which most men don't do enough of, either) isn't as difficult as it is to seek psychological help. Dealing with pain and revealing one's true fears or desires can be too uncomfortable for many men. In fact, it can be so uncomfortable that most men would rather just live with the depression than deal with the pain. To them, the cure is more painful and frightening than the disease. Still, as I did, they need to realize that the pain of the cure eventually gives way to relief. They must also realize, as I did, that the disease doesn't fix itself or get bored with you and move on.

Men also need to learn a valuable lesson about crying. I learned that crying and releasing tears was necessary, and I mean physically necessary. It is required, chemically, in order to flush all of that pain out of your soul. It helps you see clearly again. For me, it was a healthy experience. It's what God designed our bodies to do. Suppression of these emotions is unhealthy.

Why do many men see crying as anything other than a normal bodily function? Many men avoid crying because of the fear of what others will think of them. Men, like women, were not designed to live without emotion. Yet many men feel, even today, that it is acceptable for women to cry but not men. Perhaps that's why many men still feel shame for being depressed. Thankfully, some of the stereotypes are changing. Even Howard Stern, the man who has everything and seemingly has it all together, goes to therapy. I watched an interview with Stern and, admittedly, was surprised to hear that America's shock jock attended therapy four times a week. His devotion to his work left him isolated from the rest of the world. He said he had hardly any friends and had become disconnected from society. He goes to therapy because he realized that his father's closed-off feelings had rubbed off on him, and he doesn't want to pass that disconnection on to his own children. Stern's story is a perfect example that fame and enormous wealth don't automatically translate to happiness.

For me, recovery was a combination of medication, therapy, and coaching. The medication was used to get my emotions under control. Anxiety is often defined as unproductive mental energy. I had lost control of my thoughts and I needed something that would allow my mind to relax. My inability to relax led to fatigue from a lack of sleep and it further fueled obsessive thinking. Anxiety causes over-stimulation of the mind. That's why calming down became so difficult for me.

My best friend, Eric, shared an interesting Harvard University case study from the 1990s. The study concluded that a typical American performs his or her life about 60 times more productively than someone from the 1920s. Think about that – 60 times. And technology has boomed again since that study. We constantly have our cell phones at our side so we can use the Internet or email or text. We are all about instant communication and time efficiency. We conduct our lives at an incredible pace compared to our predecessors.

But Eric believes our society has become over-stimulated. Brilliant minds have contributed to an amazing evolution in technology, but maybe our minds haven't evolved at the same pace. This causes stress and duress which can result in anxiety. So the Harvard study suggests we have gone from the Great Depression of economics (1920s) to the Great Depression of the mind. It's an interesting theory.

To combat this over-stimulation, we often seek medication. I know that medication played a vital role in calming my mind. But I also needed therapy to discover what my emotional triggers were. Today's medication did wonders for my condition but I wanted to come up with an exit strategy. In order to do that, I needed to get to the root of what was hurting me and setting off anxiety (therapy) and design a plan of action to get on with my life (coaching).

Balancing My Pies

In April of 2006, two Kansas City journalists, Jeff Passan and Matt Fulks, had caught wind of my ordeal the previous year and asked if they could write stories. After gaining encouragement and some needed momentum from others who shared their struggles with me, I saw this as a rare opportunity to share my journey with others. I was far removed from any shame connected to 2005 – but there is always a risk when someone opens their life publicly for the world to see. Nevertheless, I believed if one other person gained strength from my story and began a journey toward his or her own heart, it was worth the risk.

The feedback from the stories was overwhelmingly positive. I still have a pile of letters and cards from complete strangers who wrote to thank me for being so transparent. I assumed they either gained strength from my story because of their own challenges, or they knew someone else who was suffering and my words helped them understand what a friend or loved one was enduring. Several radio and television appearances followed. I was invited to speak at several different venues. The speaking engagements created a new challenge for me. Wherever I was invited, I almost always asked the audience if there was anything they wanted me to speak about. Mostly, people wanted me to tell my story. But they also wanted to know how I have kept myself mentally and spiritually healthy since my ordeal of 2005. This was something I had put into practice but not necessarily into words.

Two things came to mind: First, thanks to work with Gary and Focus, I had learned how I had wrongly defined and wrongly applied intimacy. I had since created new, intimate relationships in my life, in the true sense of the word. Intimacy now meant to be known. I've also heard intimacy described in simple syllables, as "in-to-me-see." Especially for men, my message needed to include this new definition and new use of intimacy in my life. Secondly, I had discovered that there was an imbalance in my life. Obviously I had a chemical imbalance that led to my irrational thinking and eruption of emotions.

Exercising healthy intimacy involves balancing our P.I.E.S. (physical, intellectual, emotional, and spiritual).

Still, there was an imbalance in how I was investing my heart and my time and what made me feel alive and fulfilled. I had eliminated many emotional and physical pollutants and replaced them with healthy practices that worked for me. Without much thought, I knew my well-being was a combination of new forms of intimacy and a balance in my life. I came up with a name for my new approach: Balancing My Pies.

I had discovered through conversations, reading, and my own experience that there are four essential forms of intimacy: physical, intellectual, emotional, and spiritual. Furthermore, I discovered that each form of intimacy needed to be nourished equally. Imagine an Italian chef balancing four pizzas at once. He has one spinning on each hand, one on top of his head, and one on top of a foot. The other foot is on the ground to keep him from falling. In order to make this trick work (literally or figuratively), the chef needs to maintain the spin of each pizza or, as some refer to them, each pie. Exercising healthy intimacy involves balancing our P.I.E.S. (physical, intellectual, emotional, and spiritual).

Physical intimacy was never an issue with me in terms of seeking it, giving it, or receiving it. I come from a family that is always showing physical affection. However, I have encountered people that are very uncomfortable with physical contact. There might be some legitimate reasons for this behavior (coming from an unaffectionate family, physical/sexual abuse or rejection) but turning away from this important form of intimacy is unhealthy. In today's world, unfortunately, physical intimacy implies sexual intimacy, which is not necessarily the case. Sexual intimacy perhaps is the ultimate form of physical intimacy but certainly not the only form. A good, firm, genuine handshake is a form of physical intimacy. Couples cuddling or holding hands, parents holding hands with their children, and people walking arm and arm are all forms of physical intimacy. People giving each other a two-arm, tight hug is a healthy way of physically being known. Have you ever offered a friendly hug to an appropriate person and then been surprised with an even bigger hug in return? It feels good because we are designed to experience and enjoy physical touch. Even athletes congratulate each other by touching each other in the form of high fives. It has long been thought that foster babies that are physically handled (i.e. those that experience physical intimacy) have a better chance at survival than those that are simply fed and attended to. The suggestion is clear: We were designed to be appropriately touched and to appropriately return touch.

Intellectual intimacy was an issue for me as a young child and adolescent. My mother is an extremely well-read, well-informed, articulate woman. She speaks two languages and has a passion for world political history. Her intelligence was way too much for me to handle. She would often have people over to our house to talk politics over a bottle of wine. Great debates and arguments would break out. She was very passionate about her position on certain issues and refused to lose a debate without a fight. She was also an English major in college and ironed out every wrinkle in my speech pattern beginning with my first goo-goo-ga-ga. I was more into sports. I enjoyed time with my Dad talking about certain baseball and football players and debating who was the fastest, strongest, and best. While my Mom was always a fan of the game of baseball, having an "intellectual" conversation about sports was beneath her. That was recreational stuff; she wanted to talk about things that mattered. Because of that, I avoided any talk about the world and my grades in history, social studies, and English suffered. It wasn't until I became interested in broadcasting that I realized the importance of effective grammar skills. I never paid really close attention to the details of our country and the world until after college. In the end, I ended up being a lot more like my Mom than my Dad but my intellectual needs as a child, as trivial as they may have seemed, were not met. I had very little intellectual validation as a child.

As far as Emotional intimacy, I was both lacking and excessive. As is the case with many males in the United States of America, I didn't want my emotions to be seen as a weakness. Men aren't supposed to cry and I held in a lot of tears until 2005. Our bodies are designed to experience and express emotions. This is why a venting session feels like releasing a heavy load, a good cry feels like a release, and a belly laugh relieves stress. We experience an emotion and there is a need for this emotion to be expressed or released. I have often suggested that expressing emotion is as physically required as blowing your nose or using the restroom. Here's a graphic illustration: a man named Phil has to urinate but he refuses to relieve himself. Naturally, this causes considerable discomfort, so he reaches for a pain reliever and finds temporary relief. Not long after, the pain returns and the pain reliever has little or no effect. Now his urinary tract and bladder are feeling the strain, and an infection occurs. This poor gentleman is prescribed an antibiotic to treat the infection which helps some of the symptoms. Because of the infection, he develops a fever and has to increase his consumption of fluids. This helps lower the fever to a certain degree but now the bladder can't hold anymore fluid and the problem backs up into his kidneys. Soon he is experiencing kidney failure and his body is unable to properly remove chemicals and toxins, and on and on. I believe denying our bodies the ability to express or expel emotions creates a similar and equally as dangerous logjam. Emotions are stored and backed up, creating other issues. So when stress arrives, some of us turn to alcohol, drugs (prescription and/or recreation), smoking, excessive exercising and dieting to treat the symptoms. But the problem isn't fixed. If Phil would simply go to the restroom and empty himself, his issues would drastically improve. In terms of emotions, we all need to empty ourselves.

My life was a combination of repressing my emotions in front of some people and showering my emotions on others. If I felt someone truly cared (or was willing to listen) to how I felt, I would carry on about how I felt until I wore that person out. My opportunity for release was so limited, I often just talked and talked and talked to that unsuspecting friend. Then I would call that person every time I was blue, and would repeat the process. This was unbalanced behavior and not healthy.

Spiritual Intimacy can be a complicated ordeal or it can be quite simple. As we all know, organized religion has become a divisive subject in our culture and has led to an unseemly amount of conflict and bloodshed around the world. Because of these conflicts between different faiths and because of conflicts within the same faiths, many people have understandably, but unfortunately in my mind, walked away from the great value of spiritual intimacy. But remember, spiritual intimacy and religious intimacy are not necessarily one in the same.

I am of the Christian faith and had been a regular churchgoing person for most of my adult life. I feel I had gained much-needed wisdom and hope because of that. Still, my spiritual life was quite shallow until I decided I wanted to have a relationship with God. When Cardinal Joseph Ratzinger was ordained Pope Benedict XVI, he immediately reminded Christians of two very important things: God is love and that He desires a friendship with His children. Those were very profound words because I needed to be reminded that my creator put me on this planet as an act of love. Just like my parents want the best for me, my heavenly father desires the same. Furthermore, He wants a relationship with me. In order to have a fulfilling relationship for both sides, communication must exist. Our closest family and friends are people whom we can talk to about anything. We desire their counsel, and provide the same for them. I needed to stop assuming that God was constantly in my midst and start acting as if He actually was. Just like a good friend, I needed to make time each day to express my concerns and desires and I needed to take the time to hear the response, whenever that might come. I had made the mistake so many times in my life of praying, praying, and praying that I never let my friend get a word in edgewise. It's as if God was ready to give me His wisdom but He kept getting cut off because I wouldn't shut up and listen. Most importantly, I needed to believe that I am not in total control of my life and the circumstances around it. I am not God. There is a master orchestrator that has a plan for me, much too complicated for me to figure out on my own. I also needed to understand that the answers of my prayers would come when God believed I was ready to hear them. With all of this being said, I needed to make time to allow myself to be intimate with God so that He could be intimate with me.

It is possible to experience a certain measure of peace by balancing a P.I.E. and having limited or no spiritual intimacy. But the goal of balancing our P.I.E.S. is to have total and complete peace with ourselves and with the One that designed us with great precision and love. There is a reason that the acronym falls into place the way it does: we need to go a little deeper with each level…

P to I to E to S…

I've always felt the journey to our own heart is a journey toward God. Once we begin to appreciate how lovingly and uniquely we have been designed, it's so much easier to connect with the designer. I believe a withdrawal from our heart is equivalent to a withdrawal from God, and a withdrawal from God is a withdrawal from ourselves, in some form or another.

The same theory holds true for everyone, non-Christian or non-religious alike. It is important to have an intimate relationship with whatever you believe is your spiritual origin or destination. That is spiritual intimacy.

So what happens when we don't have our P.I.E.S. balanced? Imagine a grassy front yard in the shape of a square. Four sprinkler heads are equally spread to keep the lawn watered. When all of the sprinkler heads are functioning, the lawn flourishes.

But what happens when one sprinkler breaks and is shut-off?

That area will suffer and begin to slowly die. Meanwhile, the other three sprinkler heads will experience increased water pressure. Then another sprinkler head goes out. Now the remaining two heads are trying to manage twice their normal pressure and trying to reach the areas that aren't getting enough water. Do you see the parallel? When I decided to shut down my emotional intimacy and severely constrict my spiritual intimacy, I created an overload in the physical and intellectual departments. Pumping more water through the physical and the intellectual squares wasn't nourishing enough and I couldn't pump enough anyway, as hard as I tried, to satisfy the voids I had created in my emotional and spiritual worlds. If someone is an absolute workaholic and simply can't get away from thinking about or talking about work, this magnified intimacy is a result of something else being shut-off. It isn't because they are incredibly dedicated – it's more of a case of tying all of their self-worth into one facet of their life because it's the only way they will allow themselves to experience intimacy. It doesn't matter how successful they may become, it will never be enough because they don't realize that their drive isn't about their work, it's about hoping their devotion to this one area will cover for other voids.

Men who claim that they can't control their sex drive are an example of some one overloading his physical intimacy because the other intimacies are lacking. As sacrilegious as it may sound, I believe some people also overload their spiritual basket. Have you ever met someone who cannot express an opinion without quoting scripture? How about someone who is unable to express the desires of their heart without constantly referencing God's will? Is that what God created us to be...wind-up dolls with no soul? What about free will? I do believe that spiritual intimacy is the place to begin but I don't believe it is the only place. Otherwise God wouldn't have created a world community.

So how can we create and maintain balanced P.I.E.S. in our life? The first step is to recognize where the deficiency exists. If life isn't working for you and you feel like something is missing, you're correct. Ask yourself: "Am I willing to truly be known physically, emotionally, intellectually, and spiritually? What can I create in my life to enhance intimacy in all four departments?"

I learned in 2005 that I needed to establish several relationships with people with whom I could share my feelings without shame. If I discovered that I couldn't have that type of intimacy with a particular person, then I knew that relationship was limited. I still have productive visits with Dale, my therapist, and I rely on her expertise. But she's not my only outlet. This doesn't suggest that I have eliminated all of my friends who aren't comfortable with emotional intimacy. I'm just more aware of my boundaries. I can have intellectual intimacy with some friends but not others. Some are great for sharing emotional and spiritual intimacy but not intellectual intimacy. The best friends are the ones I share the most intimacies with but that doesn't mean I would drop my other friends. I needed to take inventory and see where I was falling short and how I might enhance an existing relationship or create something new.

Intimacy can't be faked. Trying to create intellectual intimacy about something you have no passion for will not provide effective results. Yes, it is a good practice to engage ourselves with others by discussing what makes them tick but at some point we need to express what makes us feel alive. In his great book, Wild at Heart, John Eldridge says this beautifully: "Don't ask yourself what the world needs. Ask yourself what makes you come alive, and go do that, because what the world needs is people who have come alive." Being a good friend by providing a shoulder to cry on is a noble thing. But being the never-ending shoulder to cry on doesn't work in the long run. At some point each of us needs to visit someone else's shoulder even if there is no need for tears.

The more we turn away from our own intimate needs, an important part of our soul is choked and begins to die. Physical intimacy wasn't designed to be expressed without love. Do you know of someone who "can't get enough?" That's because physical intimacy without love has an emptying effect. Someone who has had numerous physical relationships runs into two problems: they have usually boarded up and abandoned one or more of their P.I.E.S. and have confused sexual pleasure with physical intimacy. Instead of feeling fulfilled by sex, each relationship without love creates a void and the pattern continues with the distorted belief, "I guess I haven't found the right one yet." This is no different from the individual who goes from one job to the next and can't seem to find an agreeable career. Each new job is temporary relief for the symptom. The problem is pursuing jobs that aren't fulfilling. In the end, this also is an emptying practice.

When I feel like something isn't balanced in my life, I reflect on how I am spending my time, whom I am spending that time with, and what is missing. This is no different than the four food groups. It doesn't matter how much meat and grains I eat, it won't make up for the lack of fruits and vegetables and dairy I've neglected. I'm eventually going to have to return to a balanced diet or there will be consequences.

Getting Help

The life-saving step I took when anxiety and depression overwhelmed me came when I finally chose to talk to someone about it. First, it was my Mom and then two friends, and that led me to therapy with Dale Williamson. I now realize how important it was for me to stop burying my thoughts and feelings and just talk to someone. Talking about your issues is absolutely vital. Talking about my condition was the best way to begin because holding it in was no longer an alternative.

Just by calling my mother on the morning of August 8, 2005, I began a chain of events that resulted in my recovery. My mother demanded I call someone who could refer me to a professional counselor. I called my chiropractor who referred me to Dale Williamson. My meeting with Dale revealed some deeply rooted fears that I was able to address. After scraping together enough courage to meet with Dale, I had lunch, albeit hesitantly, with Robert Rogers. Robert wouldn't allow me to marginalize my pain even though I didn't feel my pain compared to his. By sharing my struggle with Fred White, I was reassured that I had the support of the Royals. Fred's acceptance gave me the courage to share my story with others. They made me feel like I wasn't alone and encouraged me to give medication a chance to help my recovery. I also stepped out of my shell and asked Fr. Tierney to anoint me, which gave me a new sense of peace. This new peace gave me the strength to reengage with society and to follow through to be emcee for TLC. The TLC event put me face-to-face with Linda Armstrong Kelly, whose words helped put me on an airplane and eventually place my wounded inner child in the arms of my mother. Once my inner child felt the comfort of his mother, I was able to open up to my mother in a way that was cleansing for both of us. This cleansing allowed me to attend weddings in Minnesota and Florida. By attending the weddings I was reminded how far my friends Dave and Gordy had come. This brought a new sense of hope to life inside of my once empty soul. Hope kicked me into another gear. I needed to start living my life instead of putting everything on hold as I waited for someone else to fulfill me. I was reminded of my own free will and the importance of moving from being a tough man to being a brave man. A tough man is afraid of fear. A brave man acknowledges his fear and thereby conquers his fear.

By being brave I shared my story with many friends. Instead of scaring them away, as I initially feared, they rallied around me and offered support I never could have imagined. Of course I never would have realized this support if I had played it like a tough man. I created new intimacy in my life. Suddenly I felt truly known. No longer was I surrounded by people who knew me by mind and flesh. I was creating a community of friends and family who knew my heart; the voice of my inner child. A friend suggested I give Gary Kuzmich a call and the growth continued. Through Gary I discovered the strength, not the weakness, in being vulnerable. We enter the world vulnerable and we depart the same as proven to me by the infants and the elderly at John Knox Village. Suddenly I recognized the value in my experience and began to exercise my vulnerability to minister to high school students.

So, a heartfelt phone call to my mother on August 8, 2005, began an amazing chain reaction. The journey continues. I continue to recover from anxiety and Major Depressive Disorder, but I haven't been cured. Like a person that changes his diet and exercises to lower his cholesterol, the maintenance continues. That same person doesn't see a lower cholesterol count as a license to sit on the couch and eat fried foods. I had to reprogram myself. I needed to be purified, but I'm not perfect. Those two words are often confused. Purification is the process of returning to the origin, which includes imperfections. Another way to describe being purified is a process of un-learning behaviors we have decided to take on. These aren't behaviors we were born with. They are learned intentionally and unintentionally. In the end, however, we decide whether we want to continue hauling them around.

Perhaps the most important decision I decided to make during my ordeal was to no longer consider myself a victim. As I have studied others who have experienced the same darkness I did, the most significant decision is whether we decide to look forward or continue to look back. As I discussed earlier in the book, there were times I felt victimized as a child (not sexually or physically). As I began to learn more about some of the differences between recovery and stagnation, I realized that victimization is either a part of a person's life experience or it is the lord of their life. Robert Rogers taught me a valuable lesson about victimization during our lunch back on August 9, 2005. Pain comes in different doses, but pain is pain. Whether it is Rogers' pain – losing his family – or our pain, it is all real. How long we decide we are going to be a victim is directly related to how long we will allow ourselves to be dragged down by our traumatic experience. With this in mind, it made no sense to detail all of my childhood pain, and therefore expose my parents' shortcomings. The bottom line is that my parents did the best they could. They weren't perfect, but neither was I.

So I decided I was going to move forward and create something new in my life. Sure, the pain of my childhood is part of who I am, but it's not the lord in my life.

When you have a broken leg, you don't dwell on how the leg was broken. You go to the doctor and take the first steps toward its healing. I'm not going to sit at home and continually blame the circumstances that led to my ailment. I want to move forward. I can't say that I enjoyed my pain in 2005, but I now see the value of experiencing it. I never would have learned all that I did about myself if I had continued to avoid my wounded inner child. Do I want to go through it again? Absolutely not. Would I be able to experience the joy I feel today without my bout with depression? Absolutely not.

In order to grow from a situation like mine, I had to take the first step. It happened when I finally became too drained emotionally to carry on. It was my personal moment of bottoming out, sitting in a closet, in the dark, sobbing uncontrollably.

My hope is that this story will be helpful to others. Put away any shame you may feel and go ahead and talk to others. If you need to, get help. You will be better because of it. Stay close to hope.

EPILOGUE

So many people came to my rescue in 2005. You have read some of the examples. My step-father, Jim McKenna, supported me by giving my Mom emotional support so that she could take on the full-time job of caring for me. Kevin Seitzer and his wife, Beth, checked in on me regularly. Their marriage embodied exactly what I was searching for in a lifetime relationship. Kevin's faith in God's timeline is something I think about often. He gave me inspirational music I still listen to when I need a lift. I shared my ordeal with the men at my weekly Bible study and listened to each one of them individually shower praise on me and personally ask God to show me the way. There was great encouragement from my best friend, Eric Von Slagle. Fred White called me at least twice a week to check on my mental well-being and offer his encouragement. Kelly Hall sent me the P.U.S.H. story. Mark Nasser was always there to talk and remind me how important it was to appreciate the here and now, and not what might or might not happen in the future. Michael Sweeney always reminded me that God's plan is always better than our own. He said he was convinced God was allowing me to go through all of this because He was preparing to bless me in ways I couldn't imagine. He was so right. I read the scriptures Robert Rogers sent me daily. Shireen Gandhi was always there when I needed a lift. She admired me for not giving up on my dreams and following my heart. My buddy, Scottie Pakulski, said he was excited for what was ahead and praised me for staying true to myself. Another close friend in Minnesota, Tom Green, believes that life tends to come to us when we take it easy on ourselves and return to our heart's desire. My brother Travis called to give me someone to talk to. On that subject, Julee Dugan made herself available for several venting sessions. My newly married friends Gordy Gutowski, Dave Dover, and Darren Schwankl called to tell me they were keeping my intentions in their prayers. Ty Jones reminded me what a good person I am and that I should never forget that.

Nate Bukaty's encouragement was to simply say, "I'm not worried about you." Dave and Carla Witty shared the same sentiment.

Kerry Ann Wells came along when I needed someone to get me out of the house.

She told me I was one of the strongest people she knew. How I needed to hear that after feeling so weak.

Jeffrey Flanagan encouraged me to put this story on bookshelves and transformed my words into this story. Fr. Paul Turner, an accomplished author, was one of the first to read my original manuscript and offer his editorial expertise.

Joe Posnanski, Dawna Grigsby, Thomas Jewitt, and Josh Lewin all read early drafts of this material and gave me valuable feedback.

Without knowing who her husband would be at the time, Sarah Hight felt compelled to pray often for her future husband in the summer and fall of 2005. Two-and-a-half years after August 17, 2005, she and I walked down the aisle together.

Most of all, I thank God for answering my prayer of purification and holding my hand throughout this journey.

Biographies

Photo courtesy of Chris Vleisides

Ryan Lefebvre is a broadcaster for the Kansas City Royals. A three-time all-Big Ten outfielder from the University of Minnesota, Ryan was drafted by the Cleveland Indians in 1993 in the 27th round.

An active member in the Kansas City community and with The Footprints Foundation, Ryan is the founder of Gloves for Kids, which raises money for youth programs in Kansas and Missouri. Ryan and his wife, Sarah, reside in Lake Winnebago, Missouri.

Courtesy of Janet Rogers Photography

Jeffrey Flanagan, also a graduate of the University of Minnesota, was an award-winning reporter and sports columnist at The *Kansas City Star* for 19 years, covering the Kansas City Royals and the Kansas City Chiefs. He also was a reporter with the *Arizona Republic* and the *Decatur* (Illinois) *Herald and Review.*

Jeffrey also authored a baseball instructional book *Lau's Laws on Hitting.* He resides in Kansas City, Missouri.